POWER TOOLS

BREAKING THE CHAINS THAT BIND YOU TO THE PHYSICAL PLANE.

Copyright © 1995 Hallie Deering

All rights reserved.
No part of this book may
be used or reproduced in any manner
whatsoever without prior written permission from
the publisher, except in the case of brief
quotations embodied in critical
reviews and articles.

Cover art by
The Divine Mother
through Hallie Deering

ISBN 0-929385-63-2

Published by
Light Technology Publishing
P.O. Box 1526
Sedona, AZ
86339

ॐ

Printed by
MISSION POSSIBLE
Commercial
Printing
P.O. Box 1495
Sedona, AZ 86339

Do-It-Yourself
POWER TOOLS

ANGELIC TECHNOLOGY
MANIFESTING ON EARTH

Channeled through
Hallie Deering
for
THE ANGEL ACADEMY

Published by
Light Technology Publishing
Sedona, AZ

OTHER BOOKS FROM THE ANGEL ACADEMY

LIGHT FROM THE ANGELS

Fascinating angelic teachings on a variety of vital metaphysical topics. Includes many advanced techniques for healing, meditation, and self-transformation that work extremely well with Power Tools, plus dozens of simple things you can do to enrich your spiritual life.

Available from Light Technology
Box 1526
Sedona, AZ 86339
(520) 282-6523

About the Channel

Prior to 1973 Hallie Deering taught at Colorado State University and the University of Colorado while she worked on her M.A. degree and a Ph.D. However, in January of 1973 when the comet Kahoutec passed near the Earth she underwent a sudden, profound psychic and spiritual awakening and almost immediately afterward found herself linked telepathically with the Angels. Within a short time circumstances brought her to Sedona, where she began an intensive course of inner metaphysical study with the Divine Mother and the Rose Angels. During her Sedona years she has undergone several difficult spiritual initiations; taught metaphysical workshops on both the physical and the astral planes; performed hundreds of crystal balances and past life regressions for lightworkers; as well as channeled, designed, and assembled over 6000 Power Tools for professional healers around the world. She currently teaches/channels several Angel Academy sessions per year on behalf of the Rose Angels. When she is not conducting the Angel Academy she lives in almost total seclusion, channeling books, Power Tools, and visionary artwork for the Divine Mother and the Angels. She also writes a regular monthly column called *Angel Voices* for the *SEDONA Journal of EMERGENCE*.

CONTENTS

I.   **THE ANGEL ACADEMY** 1
II. **ALL ABOUT POWER TOOLS** 5
      Holographic Thought Forms
      The Images
      How Power Tools Are Brought to Earth
      Choosing a Light Source
      Using Power Tools
      Caring for Power Tools
      A Few Tips
      Purchasing Power Tool Books
III. **SUPPLIES AND ASSEMBLY** 15
IV. **TEN POWER TOOL TEMPLATES** 21
V.   **DETAILED INSTRUCTIONS FOR EACH DISK** . 33
    1. The Inner Eye Disk 35
    2. The Rainbow Disk 41
    3. The Light Weaver Disk 47
    4. The Grounding Disk 53
    5. The Magnet Disk 57
    6. The Pink Rose Disk 63
    7. The Red Poppy Disk 69
    8. The Exterminator Disk 75
    9. The Michael Disk 81
   10. The Isis Disk 87

THE ANGEL ACADEMY

Power Tools are channeled to the earth plane through the Angel Academy. What is the Angel Academy, and where is it located?

In the crystal-clear energy of the finer planes one can sometimes catch a glimpse of the exquisite angelic City of Light shining with overwhelming splendor. The sight of it warms the heart and lifts the spirit. Within the Radiant City is a wondrous University, which is built of colored marble, quartz, and all manner of gemstones.

The University is overseen by the Divine Mother and run by the Rose Order of Angels. The Divine Mother is truly the Eternal, Greatly Beloved Mother of us all. The Rose Angels are incarnations of love and wisdom who serve the Divine Mother: they are almost always healers and teachers. The Rose Angels' auras look like huge flames which constantly flash a thousand shades of bright rose and gold light, while their inner forms are beautiful beyond description.

Congregated at the University are Spiritual Masters and their student initiates from all walks of life, from all the various peoples of the Universe, from all dimensions. They are here in the spirit of peace and harmony, for the purpose of attaining true wisdom and using that knowledge to help mankind and their various home worlds. In 1995 the Angelic University opened a small extension on the physical plane in Sedona, Arizona among the many powerful vortex energy fields.

The extension is called the Angel Academy, and it meets in Sedona several times a year. There is a general AngelFire Session aimed at getting students and healers strongly connected with their Angel Guides, and a Crystal Camp Session which deals with the fine angelic art of using crystals and gems for personal spiritual advancement and for healing purposes. The Master Key Session offers simple but profound angelic meditation and mind travel techniques designed to greatly strengthen your links with the finer planes and most especially with the University and its celestial staff. The Master Key Session also teaches many highly advanced mental healing techniques.

Each student works with the Divine Mother, a special Angel Companion, and one or more spiritual Masters. Every session is intensive, lasting five days from 9 a.m. until 9 p.m.

Afternoons are spent in the vortices practicing what has been learned. In addition, each student makes two special Power Tools with his or her Angel Companion, and pairs up with a classmate in order to work on each other with Power Tools and crystals. There is also free time, for meals and shopping in Sedona's metaphysical stores.

Evenings fly by as students share the day's happenings and insights with each other. In this way each person benefits from the experiences of every member of the class, which allows everyone to learn at an accelerated rate.

While students sleep at night, their Angel Guides release them from the physical body and take them traveling on the astral plane.

At the completion of each session every student is presented with an Angel Academy Certificate of Achievement, suitable for framing in the home or place of spiritual work.

A Few Details

The tuition for each Academy session is $500 per five-day class, plus $50 for an Angel TookKit, which contains the books and supplies needed to make Power Tools and carry out class assignments. Over 60% of the Angel Academy's profits go to various charitable foundations which better our spiritual lives, fight for animal rights, work to save the planet's ecology, and help the poor, the starving, and the dying. The other 40% goes toward computer equipment, publishing, advertising, conference room rental, salaries, and class supplies.

Read All About It

A very exciting 16-page full color booklet on the Angel Academy is now available. If you are meant to attend the Academy, you will know it when you see the booklet: angelic energy literally pours off every page, and those who are the most ready for the experience will feel as if they are receiving a personal invitation directly from the Angels. The Academy is asking $1 for this booklet, to help defray postage and the cost of printing in full color: you will find that as a spiritual document, its value is far, far higher than the $1 price.

To send for your booklet, send $1 to The Angel Academy, 2610 Jacks Canyon Road, Sedona, AZ 86351, or call (520) 284-1550.

II

ALL ABOUT POWER TOOLS

Power Tools are angelic instruments for healing, channeling, and clairvoyance. They represent a highly advanced level of mental and spiritual technology which is widely used and respected throughout the finer planes. Now this wonderful technology is being channeled from the healing Angels down to the physical dimension for the use of professional healers, channels, and anyone in metaphysics who is interested in moving at an accelerated pace.

Basically, Power Tools are flat, thick glass disks which are placed on the chakras. The quartz in the glass amplifies the energy field to such an extent that each disk acts as an interdimensional window which channels astral energies from the angelic realms. There are currently three types of Power Tools: the Metallic

Disks, the Temple Jewels, and the Holographic Disks. The Angel Academy teaches its students to make the Metallic Disks and the Temple Jewels. The Holographic Disks are now being made available to the general metaphysical public through this book.

Every holographic disk design consists of a photographic-quality scene or image in bright, semi-transparent colors: these scenes and images are solidified thought forms.

Thought Forms

As most students of metaphysics know, thoughts are very real, very forceful things . . . they can hurt, or they can heal: they can chain us down, or they can give us a spectacular mental and spiritual escape from our mundane surroundings.

Whenever we are thinking with concentration, our thoughts *literally* appear above our heads in the form of little holograms. Thought holograms are formed from the energies of the astral, mental and causal planes (the mental plane is just above the astral in terms of vibration; the causal is above the mental). These super-high-vibrational holographic manifestations of the mind's energy are called *thought forms*. As we think, a steady stream of thought forms is projected from our higher bodies: these holograms are clearly visible to many people who have inner vision.

Thought forms are extremely potent and can actually take on a life force of their own, especially when directed by a clear mind and firm will. When a thought form has been created to assist another person, it leaves the thinker's auric field and flies straight to the person it is to help: when it comes into contact with that person, it penetrates his or her aura and discharges its energy into the auric field. If the thought form is of an exceptionally high-vibrational spiritual or healing character, once it has lodged in the auric field it becomes a wonderful, dynamic force for change — protecting, defending, uplifting, balancing, healing, and energizing the recipient on every level. Angels and other spiritual Masters frequently send such sophisticated thought forms to their students for the purposes of healing, attunement, self-realization, spiritual enlightenment, and finer plane initiations.

Since our very beings are the thought forms of the Creator, it is readily apparent that healing thought forms are potentially one of the fastest, easiest, and most powerful ways to modify and evolve ourselves. This is especially true when the thought forms are produced by healing Angels. For lightworkers from the peaceful higher dimensions, Power Tools are like life-giving water in the desert, channeling specialized holographic energies from the Angels down to the Earth to help us restore our spiritual connections and our physical well-being.

The Images

Since thought itself is infinite, thought forms are equally unlimited in scope and possibility. Consequently there are many different Holographic Power Tools serving a wide variety of spiritual and metaphysical purposes. There are Power Tools that portray healing plants and herbs and carry their energy; Power Tools with geometric designs to open, balance, and tune the chakras; Power Tools with portraits of Ascended Masters and Angels; Power Tools that impact the DNA; Power Tools for reading past life memories and the Akashic Records; Power Tools for meditation and channeling; Power Tools for protection from negativity; and Power Tools for cleansing and healing the auric field as well as the physical and subtle bodies, to name just a few.

Power Tools are characterized by their accurate portrayal of the scenery and inhabitants of the physical, astral, mental and causal planes. Just how precise are these scenes? Each and every Power Tool image is edited at a resolution of 9,000 dots per square inch, which is *substantially* more detailed than thought forms produced by the human mind. In addition, each Power Tool is printed in bright, rich colors which send their healing frequency deeply into the body.

Power Tools accurately reproduce the very highest vibrations of the gems, flora, fauna, and spiritual beings portrayed on them. This means if you have a disk with a Master on it, *the Master's energy actually flows through the disk* . . . the same holds true for the healing energies of the Angels, plants, gems and everything else that is portrayed on the various Power Tools.

It should be noted that the term "Holographic Disk" does not mean that the picture itself is a hologram, but rather that the disk transfers its image into the recipient's auric field in a form of an *astral, mental, or causal* hologram.

How Power Tools Are Brought to Earth

Power Tools are channeled directly from the Divine Mother (who is of angelic origin) and a group of healing Angels who specialize in holographic thought forms. As a result of centuries of exacting study and mental discipline, these beautiful, gentle Angels are able to create very intricate, precise thought forms which radiate Divine Grace.

In order to bring the highly detailed angelic thought forms down to our physical plane, the original Power Tools were channeled from the Angels down to Hallie Deering. She then carefully reproduced each image using advanced computer technology, printed it on transparent film, and then assembled anywhere from two to four layers of transparencies by hand into disk form.

Since the above process is very exacting, tedious, and slow, only a few hundred Power Tools could be made per year for the use of those whose inner guidance led them to the disks. After a few years, however, orders were flooding in from all over the world, and it became impossible to fill them all. Finally the Rose Angels decided to discontinue the disks, because there was no way to make enough of them by hand. But the demand for them did not go away!

Eventually the Angels reached a wonderful compromise: they decided to put out books of Do-It-Yourself Power Tools which each lightworker could assemble for him/herself. Hallie Deering still channels the designs of the Power Tools, but they are printed commercially on very thin, transparent paper instead of acetate, which makes them about 80% easier to produce and assemble. This means you can buy a Do-It-Yourself Power Tool book with ten designs for a fraction of what they used to cost. In fact, the original collection of ten Power Tools in this book sold for $700. So by putting them together yourself with a few inexpensive supplies from your stained glass shop, you save a *substantial* amount of money.

These ten Power Tools have brought profound changes to many lightworker's lives; if you assemble them carefully and use them according to instructions, they can do the same for you.

Choosing a Light Source

Light plays a vital role in transferring the energy from the disks into the user's auric field. The disks are, in fact, specifically designed to be used with a strobe light, because it is the pulsating rhythm of the strobe that carries a Power Tool's image quickly and deeply into the aura. Radio Shack sells a somewhat awkward medium-sized strobe light for about $35, and a dandy small hand-held jogger's strobe for about $20. Many professional healers prefer Edmund Scientific's Strobe-Tachometer which flashes up to 8000 times per second. You can order this strobe by calling 1-609-573-6250 and asking for #671,500. The price is $149. The astonishing results a strobe produces make any of the above units well worth the investment. *Please remember, however, to never ever strobe a person with epilepsy.*

If no strobe is available, the disks are used with ordinary room light for a longer time. The average time needed to transfer a disk's image into the auric field is 2-3 minutes *with* a strobe light, or about 20 minutes *without* a strobe.

A third way to use Power Tools is to place them on a light box. Light boxes are Lemurian and Atlantean devices used to broadcast energy throughout a house, temple, or any other large space.

Using Power tools on a light box forms a vortex of astral light which completely fills a house or a healing room with angelic energy. The light box is lit for only about 60 minutes a day, usually 30 minutes in the morning and 30 minutes at night. That time is sufficient to fill your house with a column of astral light for the next 24-72 hours.

You can buy a light box at a printer's supply or a photography shop, but they are liable to be expensive. You can easily make your own, however, either simply or elaborately, depending on your taste, time and budget.

Basically you need a box with a light inside and a frosted glass top which light can shine through. For super simplicity, take the shade off a small lamp and give it a 15 watt bulb (no bigger, you don't want to risk starting a fire,) then put a large cardboard box upside down over the lamp. Cut out the top of the box (actually the bottom, since it is upside down) and cover it with a piece of white glass, available at a reasonable price at stained glass shops. Voilà: a light box. As an alternative you can gut a pair of old stereo speakers or use a wood crate or a plastic waste paper basket . . . look around and see what is handy. You can also decorate your light box with paint, contact paper, cutouts, posters, tarot cards, or whatever.

Using Power Tools

Most people feel strong bolts of energy as they hold Power Tools; when the disks are strobed on their chakras, extraordinary things begin to happen very quickly.

During a Power Tool session — especially if a strobe is being used — the image on each disk is perfectly reproduced as a hologram in the recipient's aura, where it shines with great beauty as it begins its work of healing, balancing, and energizing. Although the auric effects of one session can last for several weeks, the more times a disk is used, the more potent its effects will be as it becomes a permanent part of the recipient's aura.

Power Tools are especially wonderful in combinations. Using different disks on several or all of the chakras at the same time produces a *truly intense* healing session, helping you find, unravel, and understand every possible ramification of a problem.

Power Tools work extremely well with virtually all other healing techniques such as massage, Reiki, crystals, hands-on, psychotherapy, and the like, as well as with guided meditation tapes, flower essences, gem elixirs, aromatherapy, toning, crystal bowls, Tibetan bells, classical or New Age music, and so on.

After a deep Power Tool session using the channeled techniques that come with the disks, many people experience profound feelings of release and exhilaration, a crystal-clear state of consciousness, deepening moments of self-awareness, keen past life recall, and sometimes a rush of spiritual devotion that borders on ecstasy. In short, Power Tools are definitely the *genuine article*.

Lightworkers from many parts of the world work with Power Tools, and they all have an abundance of tales to tell about the truly profound miracles the disks have brought into their lives and into the lives of their family, friends, and clients.

Caring for Power Tools

1. *Never ever get your disks wet!* If water gets under the copper tape it can ruin the picture inside the disk.

2. Avoid placing your Power Tools in direct sunlight, which can fade the colors. The disks receive energy from the Central Sun on the astral plane and do not require physical sunlight.

3. Always hold your disks by the edges, to avoid smudging them: the Angels cannot channel astral light through a grubby disk.

4. Wipe your disk clear of smudges with a soft cloth lightly dampened with a little Windex, *being careful not to get moisture under the copper tape.* Then clean the disk vibrationally for 15-20 minutes on a Microcrystal Card or hold it for 30-60 seconds high up (to avoid burning it) in the smoke of sandalwood incense or a cedar/sage smudge stick. If you cannot find Microcrystal Cards in your local metaphysical shop, call Crystal Magic in Sedona at (520) 282-1622 or Crystal Castle at (520) 282-5910.

5. Please do not sleep with your Power Tools or carry them around all day in your pocket! Power Tools put out an ultrasonic frequency: in small doses, this ultrasound is very healing, but it can erode your etheric body if you are near your disks for long periods of time. Power Tools are designed to be used intensely for a short time, then put away in order to contain their penetrating energy field.

6. If you travel with your disk, a small inexpensive Chinese silk jewelry pouch will keep it from picking up miscellaneous vibrations.

7. When traveling by air it is best to pack your Power Tools in your check-through baggage. If you carry them on board with you, hand them past the X-ray machine if you can.

A Few Tips

1. Power Tools are used with the printed design side up, away from the body.

2. The more times a person uses a Power Tool, the stronger and more permanent its effect will become in his/her life.

3. Even if an illness is not ready to be released (because its lesson has not been learned), Power Tools can still bring a great deal of comfort and relief to the afflicted person.

4. Sometimes during a disk session tears will flow; this is a positive sign that trauma has been contacted and is being released.

5. After a Power Tool session, it will be of great benefit to both the healer and the client to soak in a hot tub (not necessarily together!) with mineral salts in order to relax and purify the physical body, and to remove the emotional and cellular debris that is usually released into the auric fields of both people.

Future Power Tool Books

Power Tool books contain the designs for ten Holographic Power Tools. They include detailed instructions on how to assemble each disk and how to use it. This is the first book: if all goes as planned, one new Power Tool book will be published each year, probably in the spring.

The Angel Academy also publishes its text book, *Light from the Angels*. This profound work contains channeled information from the Divine Mother and the Rose Angels on a wide variety of topics including healing, crystals, and meditation. The information is intended to speed up the personal evolution of lightworkers, so each of us can attain our spiritual goals quickly and safely. Many of the advanced healing and meditation techniques presented in this book can also be used to greatly enhance and expand your Power Tool work.

You may order all Angel Academy books through your local metaphysical bookstore, or through Light Technology. Call Light Technology at (520) 282-6523 to inquire about pricing, shipping and handling, and so on. Checks may be sent to Light Technology, Box 1526, Sedona, Arizona 86339.

III

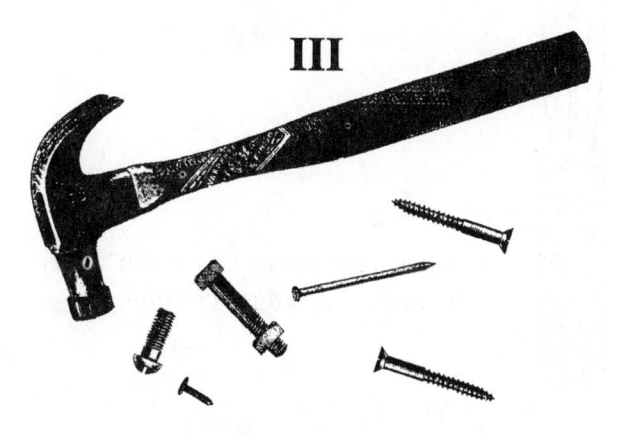

SUPPLIES AND ASSEMBLY

In order to put your Power Tools together you will need a few inexpensive supplies which can be found in almost any stained glass shop. If your local store should not have the necessary items, they can order them for you.

1. **Glass**: For each Power Tool you plan to make you will need two pieces of glass. If the Power Tool is large, ask for two **3" round glass bevels**. If the Power Tool is small, ask for two **2" round glass bevels**. This glass is round, clear, flat on one side and beveled on the other. Expect to pay about $2 per piece. Since glass contains quartz, it is the power source for your disk.

2. **Copper Tape**: One role of copper tape will make over 100 Power Tools. Ask for either a **1/4" or 5/16" wide roll of copper**

Two glass bevels with their flat faces together, seen from the side.

Copper tape, about this much wider than both glass edges combined.

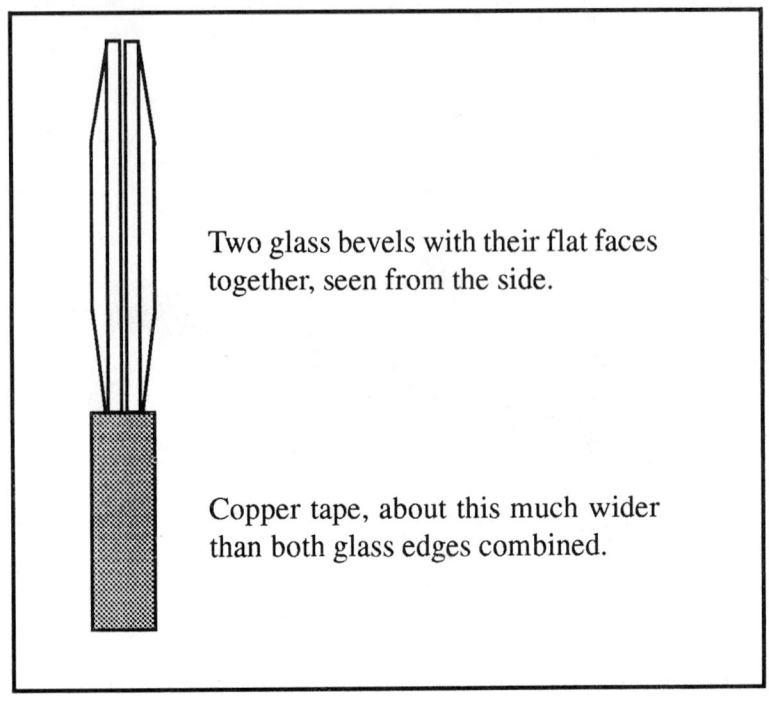

Illustration A.

foil, 1.0 mil thick. The thickness of the glass bevels can vary, so in order to determine which width is best, put the flat sides of two pieces of glass together and measure them against the width of the tape. The tape should be about 1/8" wider than the two pieces of glass (see Illustration A). A roll of copper foil costs about $5. The copper seals the energy field of the disk, and provides an electrical conduit for inflowing angelic energy.

Putting It All Together

When you have your supplies, simply follow these five easy steps.

1. **Clean** the flat sides of both glass bevels using Windex, vinegar and water, or any other non-abrasive liquid cleaning solution. Once the flat sides of the glass are clean, handle it by the edges so the glass doesn't get fingerprinted or smudged.

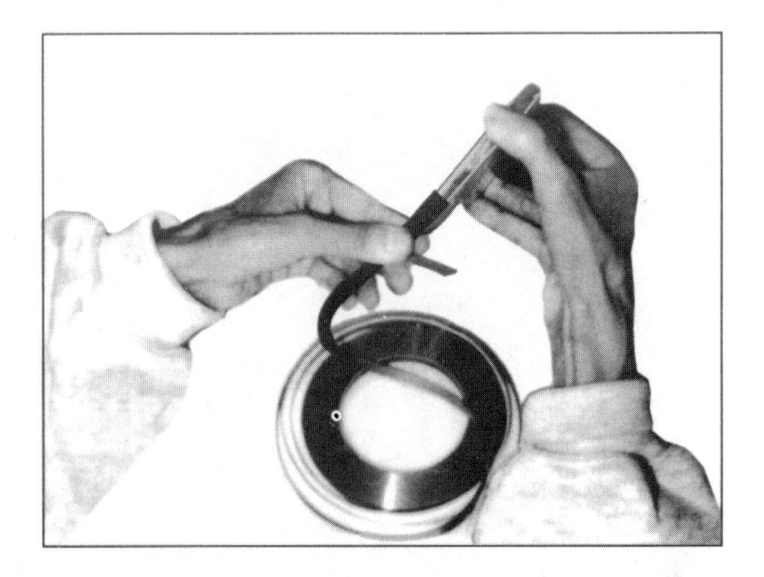

Illustration B. Holding the glass by the edges, press the copper foil down so it overlaps the glass the same amount on each side. Then slowly rotate the disk, peeling the backing away from the foil and pressing tape down onto the edge of the glass as you go. Be sure to keep the tape overlap even on each side of the glass.

2. **Cut** the Power Tool you wish to assemble out of the book. It is easiest to cut it out in a square with regular scissors and then trim it into a circle with a pair of curved fingernail scissors. Before you cut the circle, put one of the glass bevels over the design to see if the size is right. If your glass is slightly smaller than the design, compensate for this when you cut the circle. *The paper circle should not be bigger than the glass circle but it can be a tiny bit smaller.* In general, paper and glass should be as close to the same size as you can get them.

3. **Brush off** the flat faces of the glass and both sides of the paper Power Tool template to remove dust and lint. Any *soft brush* will work for this — try a makeup brush or a 1" paint brush.

4. **Assemble** the disk by making a sandwich of the glass and paper: place the paper template on the flat side of one piece of

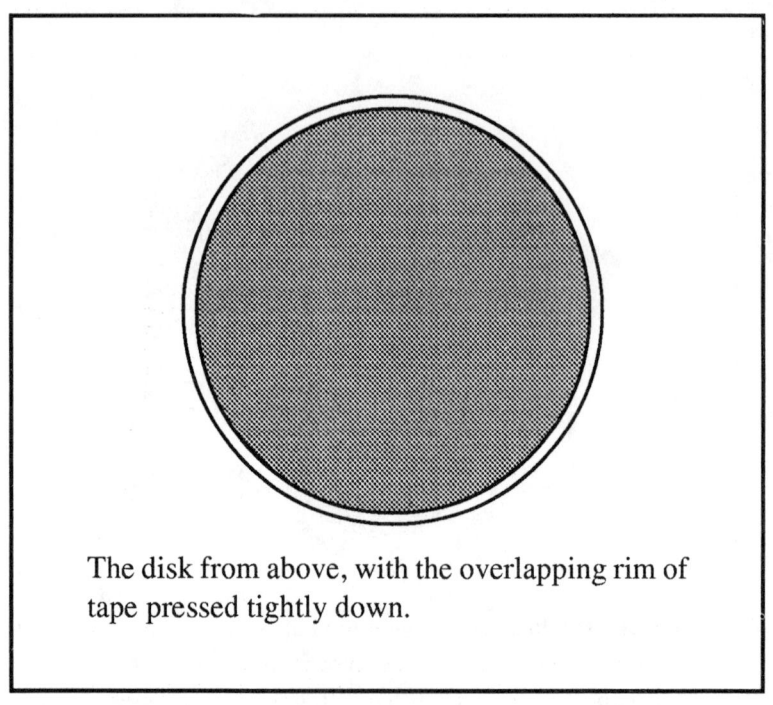

The disk from above, with the overlapping rim of tape pressed tightly down.

Illustration C.

glass, then put the second piece of glass on top of it, flat side down.

5. **Tape** the Power Tool together using the copper foil. Remove the foil from its plastic bag and set it flat on your work table. Then unstick the end of the tape and separate several inches of it from its backing.

Now pick up the Power Tool by the edges and press the copper tape onto the edge of the glass. The tape will be wider than the glass: center the tape on the glass edge so it overlaps both sides evenly. (See Illustration B.)

Slowly rotate the glass, pressing the tape onto the edge of the glass as you go. As you press the tape along the glass, separate more of it from its backing. When you have taped all around the edge and are back where you started, overlap the beginning edge of the tape by an inch or so, then cut the tape straight across and press the cut edge firmly down.

Next, hold the disk by the center with one hand (the way you would hold a hamburger), and with the index finger of your other hand press the overlapping edges of excess tape down onto the face of each glass disk, so you have a narrow rim of tape flat against each glass face (See Illustration C.) Lastly, take the side of a wood pencil or plastic pen and smooth the loose tape rims down hard, so the tape is sealed flat and tight against the face of the glass.

When your tape is well stuck, clean the front and back of your Power Tool with a slightly damp cloth to remove fingerprints and smudges. Be sure to avoid getting moisture under the tape rim.

Bingo! It is finished! Once you have made your first Power Tool the rest will be easy.

It will take your Power Tools twenty-four hours to rev up to their full energy after being assembled. Then they will be ready to use.

IV

TEN POWER TOOL TEMPLATES

**Why does
the Cheshire Cat smile?**

**Because he works with
Power Tools, that's why!
Can you find his special
Interdimensional Disk
in this picture?**

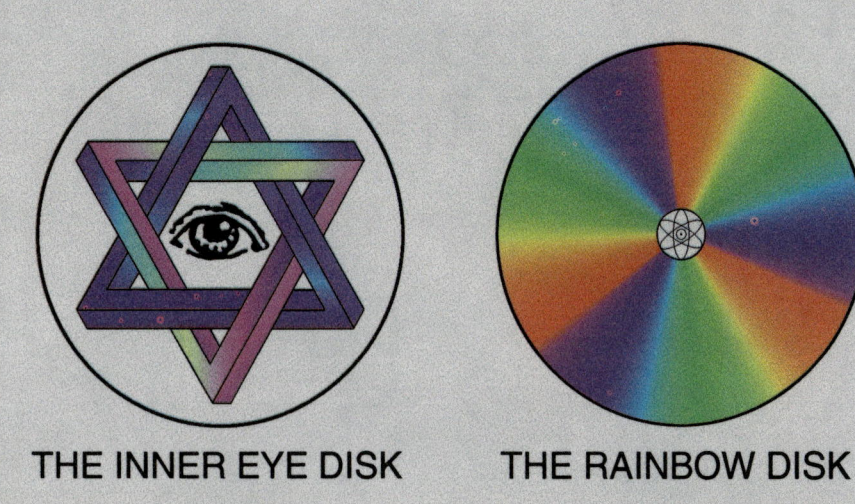

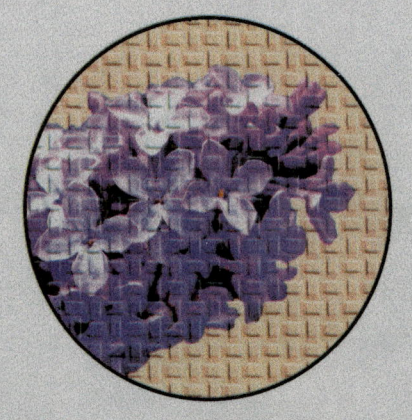

THE INNER EYE DISK   THE RAINBOW DISK

THE LIGHT WEAVER DISK   THE GROUNDING DISK

THE RAINBOW DISK

THE INNER EYE DISK

THE GROUNDING DISK

THE LIGHT WEAVER DISK

THE MAGNET DISK

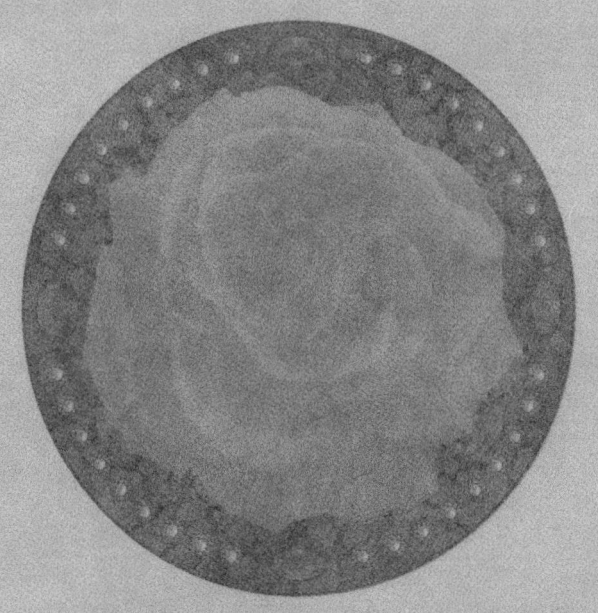

THE PINK ROSE DISK

THE MAGNET DISK

THE PINK ROSE DISK

THE RED POPPY DISK

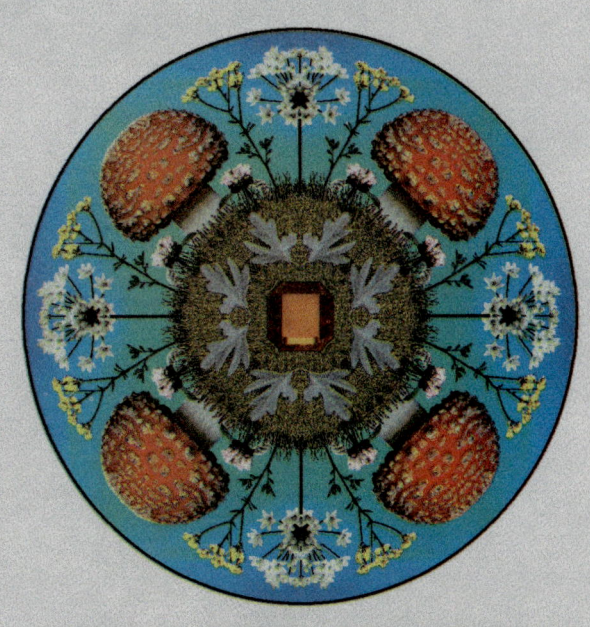

THE EXTERMINATOR DISK

THE RED POPPY DISK

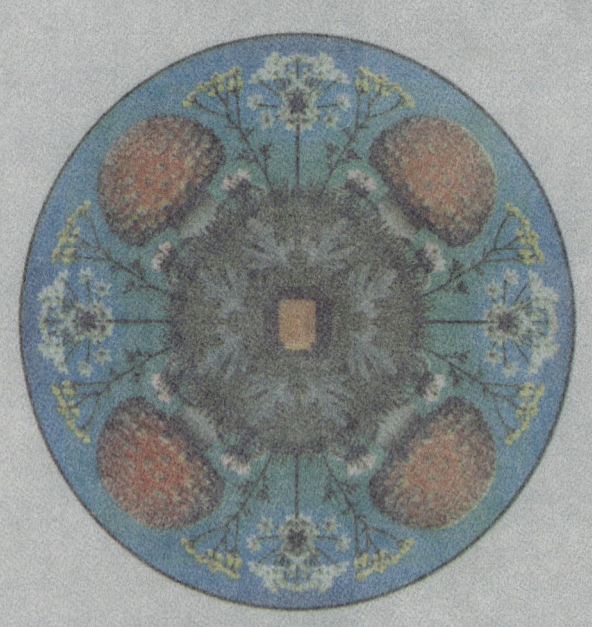

THE EXTERMINATOR DISK

THE MICHAEL DISK

THE ISIS DISK

THE MICHAEL DISK

THE ISIS DISK

V

DETAILED INSTRUCTIONS FOR EACH DISK

1

The Inner Eye Disk

The Inner Eye Power Tool balances right-left brain function, then calibrates the energies of the third eye and synchronizes them with those of another psychic eye (the fourth eye) located high on the forehead directly above the third eye.

Just as your two physical eyes working together give you three-dimensional vision, so your two non-physical eyes combine to give you fourth- and even fifth-dimensional vision.

Deep meditation with an Inner Eye Disk is like looking through a hole in a wall into another dimension. The disk emits subtle astral sounds which combine with its colors and energy circuitry patterns to literally vibrate a hole in earth's three-dimensional energy field and serve as a conduit for inflowing fourth- and fifth-dimensional energies.

Your Inner Eye Disk is sublime for meditation, thought projection, dreaming, telepathy, reading the Akashic Records, psychometry, past lives, channeling, problem solving, and so on.

Using The Disk

Like all Power Tools, Inner Eye Disks are *activated by light*. Because seeing into the finer planes is difficult, the kind of light you use with this disk is particularly important.

A small strobe light will give the best results with the Inner Eye if you wish to sit upright during your meditation, if you are meditating for only a short time, or if you are using your disk on someone else to guide them in a healing or meditation session. Place the disk over the third eye, then strobe it for no more than two minutes, holding the strobe about five inches from the disk. This will activate the disk and your third- and fourth-eye centers, preparing you for deep-level psychic work. *However, remember to never, ever use a strobe light with a person who has epilepsy.*

If you do not have a strobe or if you wish to meditate for longer than thirty minutes, lie down and use your disk on your forehead during the entire meditation in a well-lit room. Meditating or channeling in this manner will take you very, very deep.

When the disk is in place and activated by light, its colors will break the incoming light into various wavelengths. After the light is split, the lines, angles, and symbols in the disk direct the energy to various key areas of the brain, to the psychic chakras, and to the subtle bodies.

Like all Power Tools, the Inner Eyes is used on the third eye with the printed side up, away from your skin. The direction the triangles point depend on what you are doing with the disk: see the exercises below.

In order to fully activate the Inner Eye Disk and take advantage of its wide range of powers, use it in combination with the Grounding Disk and begin your first few sessions with the following exercises. At first the exercises may not be easy to do, because they are diagnostic: the ones you have difficulty with show in which way your psychic centers are imbalanced. Repeating the difficult exercises helps correct the imbalance. The more you work with your disk, the easier the exercises will become as the right and left hemispheres of your brain come into synchronization and your third- and fourth-eye chakras are energized, aligned, tuned, and focused.

The Ping-Pong Exercise

This exercise expands and equalizes the energy flow between the right and left hemispheres of the brain, and increases the energy current connecting the third- and fourth-eye chakras.

To begin, place the disk on your forehead with the eye *vertical*. One tip of the blue triangle points to the left side of your forehead, and one tip of the pink triangle points to the right side of your forehead. Be sure the disk is centered over your third eye. Now close your eyes and focus your attention inside your head just behind your physical eyes. Imagine that you are in a small room with mirrored walls, using a paddle to bounce a white ping-pong ball 25-50 times against the left wall. Then switch the paddle to your left hand and bounce the ball against the right wall 25-50 times. At first the ball may tend to travel slowly — work at making it go harder and faster, until it is traveling in a perfectly straight iine. Lastly, with the sheer power of your mind instead of a paddle, bounce the ball rapidly from one wall to the other, back and forth, about 35 times.

Next, you can use the same exercise to increase the energy flow between the third and fourth eyes. Rotate the disk so the eye is *horizontal*, with one point of the blue triangle up and one point of the pink triangle straight down. Repeat the same exercise moving the ball straight up to the center of the ceiling, then down to the center of the floor, back and forth about 25-50 times.

The Traveling Disk Exercise

This exercise is for projecting the third- and fourth-eye energies, focusing them, and using their magnifying abilities to see distant events in minute detail. It is also excellent for establishing and strengthening telepathic links with Angels, Masters, guides and friends.

Begin by placing the disk over your forehead with the eye in the *horizontal* position.

Do you remember the Slinky wire coil toy from your childhood? Close your eyes and visualize that you have a Slinky made out of gold light sitting on your forehead. Attached to the top of the Slinky is your Inner Eye Disk.

Now visualize that with the power of your mind you are spiraling the Slinky out so it pushes the mental image of the Inner Eye Disk away from you. Keep one end of the Slinky anchored on your forehead, and spiral the other end way, way out, as far as you can get it, imagining that it is pushing the Power Tool image ahead of it. Now pull the disk image back to your forehead, then spiral it out again. Push it further and further away each time. It will stretch out infinitely far . . . all the way around the planet, with practice!

Try visualizing that you are sending the image of the Inner Eye Disk in this manner to a friend's house. When it gets there, imagine that it will locate your friend and show you what he/she is wearing. Then check with your friend later to see if your impression is correct. This technique may be used to gather information or establish communication links all over the planet, *as long as you do not invade another person's privacy.* Always bring the image of the Slinky and the Inner Eye Disk back to your forehead when you are finished.

The Master Meditation Technique

This meditation method is simple, quite powerful, and with practice takes only a few minutes. It will raise your spinal energies and flood your cerebral meditation centers with psychic force.

To begin, lie down with the disk on your forehead over your third eye, or sit so you can comfortably hold the disk in place. The disk should be in its normal position with the eye horizontal, the blue triangle pointing up, and the pink triangle pointing down.

Breathe deeply and slowly through your solar plexus for about two minutes. This will prepare you for deep meditation by pulling large amounts of soul energy down into the physical body.

Next, visualize or form a strong, clear idea that you are rising up out of your physical body in a body made out of pure, rich gold light. When you are standing up in this gold body, imagine that the physical landscape is fading away, and in its place a beautiful green meadow is beginning to shimmer and take form. Fill in grass, flowers, trees, sky, birds, etc. Notice that in the center of the meadow is a large pyramid made out of brilliant white light. It has steps going up all four sides, leading to a capstone of gold light. This pyramid is about sixty feet tall, with the capstone comprising the last ten feet. Visualize that you are walking over to the pyramid in your gold body and are standing by the first step.

The point of this meditation technique is to climb the pyramid: as you climb, energy will begin to flow up your spinal column from the first (base) chakra all the way to the crown of your head. This is like raising an antenna on a radio to prepare it to receive incoming sound waves –– only in this case, you are preparing to receive incoming thought waves and spiritual vibrations.

As you begin to climb, focus on your gold legs and take high steps. Almost immediately you should get the sensation of rising . . . this tells you that the energy is beginning to flow up your spine. Climb *64 steps* straight up: with the 64th step, enter into the gold light of the capstone.

Sit down and make yourself comfortable in the capstone. Let the gold light of the capstone flow through your gold body, filling it with intense energy. You should have a feeling of having climbed to a very great height. Now take a moment to visualize an eye that fills your whole mind . . . this opens your third eye and prepares it for meditation.

From here, you can do whatever you wish. If you know other

meditation techniques, you will find that they are more profound from the top of the pyramid because you have, in effect, put your antenna up. If you don't know any other meditation techniques, try some of the following methods.

In order to receive information, you need to set up a familiar situation that your physical brain recognizes and can work with. Try visualizing that the space in the capstone is like your own private retreat, with books, photo albums, newspapers, audio tapes, a tv set, radio, telephone, computer, filing cabinets, windows and doors — and then use whichever of these suits you. For example, if you would like to scan a past life, you could visualize that you are opening a book and reading the information; hearing it narrated on a tape or radio; watching it on a tv show; bringing up past life memory files on a computer; watching the scene out a window; or walking out the door into the past life. Try all of the above methods to get whatever information you would like, then use whichever one works best.

If you would like to learn more about angelic meditation, *Light From the Angels* contains a wealth of meditations dealing with mind travel, healing, reading the Akashic Records, exploring past lives, clearing past life trauma from the DNA, and so on. Combining these techniques with the Inner Eye Disk usually gives profound results.

2

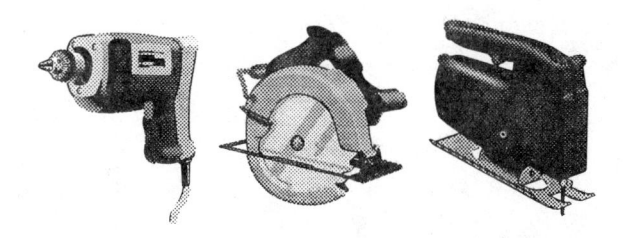

The Rainbow Disk

The Rainbow Disk is a healing tool which radiates full spectrum light frequencies. At the same time, the colors, copper, and quartz in the disk combine to produce more healing energies in the form of astral sound frequencies which are just above the normal range of hearing. This powerful combination of light and sound produces an extremely strong healing energy. Think of the Rainbow Disk as a bottle of mega-vitamins which replenish vital physical and astral energies while they tune the aura and subtle bodies.

When adverse circumstances or surfacing past life trauma cause the astral and physical bodies to lose or forget their original vibratory rate, disease begins to manifest first in the auric field and then in the physical body at the level of the atoms and molecules. The Rainbow Disk is designed to help retune the vibrations of the aura, atoms, and molecules with light and sound, thus restoring a state of health at the most basic levels.

The Rainbow Disk is also superb for opening a healer's hand chakras more than they have ever been before, and for tuning the hand energy. In addition, the disk will realign the astral body with the physical, which promotes general well-being and greatly speeds up healing.

The Colored Rays

Before using your Rainbow Disk, it would be well to familiarize yourself with some of the basic therapeutic qualities of color. There are many excellent books on the subject — Darius Dinshah's *Let There Be Light* is probably the most famous. If you have no reference books, the following brief list will get you started:

The Magenta Ray: Opens the base chakra for women, which removes stress and releases past life talents. Balances and stimulates the aura, astral body, and the emotions. A spiritual energy.

The Red Ray: Opens the base chakra for men and women, removes stress and releases past life talents. Cleansing, highly energizing, revitalizes the five sense: an aphrodisiac. Can elevate blood pressure.

The Orange Ray: Opens the second chakra, which removes stress, anger, frustration, aggression, and self-esteem problems. Promotes creativity, stabilizes emotions.

The Yellow Ray: Opens the navel chakra, relieving stress and crippling diseases. Energizes muscles, builds nerves. Fights depression.

The Lime Ray: Opens the solar plexus chakra, alleviates psychosomatic and emotional problems, releases stress, integrates emotions, strengthens the astral body.

The Green Ray: Opens the heart chakra, balances the entire body. Calms emotional extremes, brings harmony.

The Turquoise Ray: Opens the throat chakra, encourages self-expression, channeling, clairaudience, and spiritual abilities.

The Blue Ray: Opens the third eye chakra for visualization, visions, insight, inspiration, intuition. A light sedative, builds vitality.

The Indigo Ray: Opens the fourth eye chakra. For visions and spiritual insight. Eases suffering, lessens excitement and overactivity, a sedative.

The Purple Ray: Decreases sensitivity to pain. Induces relaxation and sleep. Calms violent emotions.

The Violet Ray: Opens the crown chakra for spiritual fulfillment and perception of the divine forces. A tranquilizer.

Using The Rainbow Disk

The Rainbow Disk may be used in three major ways. If your inner guidance suggests additional ways . . . try them!

1. Using the disk on the body: The Rainbow Disk may be used directly on the body, either on a problem area or on the closest chakra. Most people will find it easy to choose or channel the appropriate color combinations. (If you have difficulty, the Inner Eye Disk is excellent for this purpose.)

The Rainbow Disk is simply placed on the appropriate part of the body and "dialed" so the desired color is straight up, pointing toward the client's head. If you wish to tune the entire physical body at once, place the disk on the heart chakra with the green ray up. To tune the astral body, place the disk on the solar plexus with the lime ray up. To tune the mental body, place the disk above the crown with the violet ray up. For those who are low on physical energy, place the disk over the spleen with the violet ray up.

For even more power you may work above the disk with your hands, especially if you have used the disk to open your hand chakras (see below). Placing the center of your palm or your bunched fingers a few inches above the disk and rotating them clockwise will spiral energy into the body. Or visualize that each of your fingers radiates a different frequency, and place one finger on the center of the disk. For example, if you have dialed the red or orange ray on the disk, visualize that your index finger is flooding extra red/orange energy into the center of the disk. Try your middle finger for yellow; your ring finger for green; and your little finger for blue and violet.

You may also work above the disk with crystals, a pendulum, bells, chimes, incense, and so on.

2. Realigning the astral body: Illness, accidents, stress, pollution, loud noises, and the like all pull our astral bodies out of alignment, which leads to stress and impedes healing. When the Rainbow Disk is strobed, it will snap the astral body back into perfect alignment with the physical. To do this, place the disk on either the heart chakra with the green ray up, or on the solar plexus chakra with the lime ray up and begin strobing. When the disk appears to jump, the astral body is realigning. It may "jump" several times before the astral is where it should be.

3. Energizing the hands: Healers can use the Rainbow Disk to open and tune their hand chakras, which will cause the astral energy flowing through the hands to greatly intensify and light up like a neon rainbow.

Normally, healing energy is brought down into a healer's body through the crown chakra. The energy then flows to the heart chakra, which relays it to the hand chakras. The major hand chakras are located in the center of the palm, and the secondary chakras are at the tips of the fingers.

To fully activate your hand chakras, strobe the Rainbow Disk flat above the crown of your head for about two minutes in order to initiate the flow of healing energy down into your body. Then strobe the disk for two minutes at the heart chakra, and finish by strobing the disk flat in the center of each palm for two minutes.

When your hand chakras are activated and tuned, proceed with your normal hands-on healing method . . . the increased energy flow will last as long as you are doing your healing session. Many people can see the new energy by holding their palms over their *closed eyes* in a well-lit room.

As you are doing your healing work after opening your hand chakras, try rubbing your hands briskly together, visualizing that you are washing them in the specific color of light that you need. To heal with pure spiritual love, use your whole hand to caress deep pink or rose-colored energy into the client's body. Or try flicking your fingers rapidly above a problem area: droplets and rays of vivid color will fly off the fingers to penetrate deeply into the tissue. Using both hands to paint rainbows of light through someone's auric field will do wonders for his or her health and emotions.

If you use the Rainbow Disk frequently to open your hand chakras, you are likely to become constantly aware of this new energy flowing through your hands, even when you are not working on someone.

4. Meditating with the disk: Try putting the Rainbow Disk on your heart chakra and projecting the full color spectrum of love and healing from your heart out through the disk to someone in need, or to the planet in general.

3

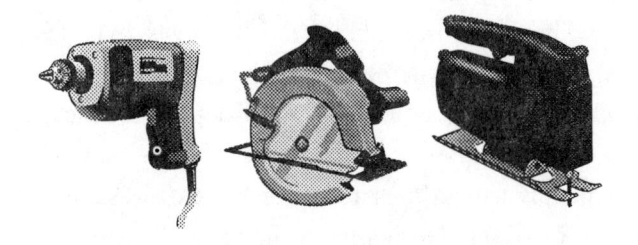

The Light Weaver Disk

The Light Weaver Power Tool provides a mending pattern for quickly and easily patching auric fields that have been damaged by holes. As it works, this Power Tool also fills the aura with the cleansing, healing, high-frequency spiritual vibration of lilac.

Almost everyone living in our stressful century can benefit from the Light Weaver. Auric holes usually result from strong negative emotions: anger, fear, grief, stress, and a state of constant worry all take their toll on the aura, as do accidents, illness, pollution, pesticides, loud noises, electrical fields, many prescription drugs, and some food additives.

Moderate use of tobacco and/or alcohol also causes leaks in the auric field, while prolonged use of these substances causes large rips in the fabric of the aura.

Even infrequent use of social drugs can tear huge holes in the aura: cocaine and heroin are especially devastating in this regard.

Why Worry About Holes?

Holes in the auric field should be of major concern to all of us. Since the aura is the immune system's first line of defense, a breach can have very serious consequences that can eventually lead to illness, insanity, or even death.

Auric holes leave corresponding parts of the physical body without their protective energy fields. These areas of the body then begin leaking life force, lose their correct vibratory frequency, and become susceptible to fatigue, invasion by germs and parasites, illness, and general malfunction.

In addition, auric holes can leave a person susceptible to negative astral energies and influences. Hallucinations experienced by people using drugs and alcohol are a classic example of this type of problem. Normally the aura shields us from perceiving unpleasant lower astral entities and thought forms, but when the auric defenses are damaged, vicious impressions, sights and sounds can flood into the conscious mind.

The subconscious mind is even more susceptible to these problems, which can frequently result in nightmares, insomnia, exhaustion and mental instability.

One of the main problems of our time is that young people (and older people as well) shatter their auras with drugs, alcohol, and loud heavy metal music. When the damage has been done, negative entities then invade the injured aura, where they cling and suck life force in a leech-like manner. Under these circumstances sleep becomes a bizarre nightmare that drains huge amounts of life force, and eventually the waking state also becomes nightmarish as more and more time is devoted to drugs or alcohol in a futile attempt to escape from it all. When the person is too exhausted to think clearly, the negative entities begin goading the victim to commit violent acts, which provide the entities with even more of the peculiar, sickening energy that they thrive on.

For all of the above reasons, healers would be well advised to routinely check every client for holes. Whether large or small, auric holes may be likened to a rip in the hull of a ship . . . under unfavorable circumstances, even a small hole can eventually sink the ship.

Detecting Auric Holes

Holes in the auric field may be located in four ways: by looking at the auric field; through meditation; by "feeling" the aura; or by an educated guess. Hole finding is best accomplished by someone other than the person with the suspected problem, since auric holes can distort perception of oneself. Whichever method you use, listen carefully to your inner guidance.

1. Looking at the aura: If you can see auras, you have an enormous advantage. Begin by standing the client in front of a white or black background, whichever is best for your auric vision. The auric field is best seen when the body is naked — if this is not possible, underwear or loose, light-colored cotton clothing will do.

Some people find it easier to see the aura with their eyes half closed, or slightly out of focus, or by looking out of the corner of their eyes.

Stand 8-10 feet from your client and scan from about 24 inches above the head down to the feet. Begin with the front of the aura, then have the client slowly turn 360 degrees. Check the back of the aura very carefully. Auric holes can appear as pale regions, as shadows, or as cloudy, smoky, black, or vacant areas.

2. Scanning the aura in meditation: Sit in a comfortable position 8-10 feet away from the client, who should be dressed as described above. Holding an Inner Eye Power Tool up to your forehead for three to four minutes before beginning will help boost your ability to detect holes.

Start with the client facing you: close your eyes and visualize a glowing white light surrounding her/him. As above, scan from the crown energy down to the feet, having the client slowly rotate 360 degrees. The difference is that in this case your eyes are closed and you are relying on your inner vision to show you defects in the aura. The holes will appear to your psychic sight as dark grey or black clouds against the luminous light of the auric field.

3. Feeling The Aura: With a little patience, the aura is surprisingly easy to feel. As always for auric work, the client should be naked or dressed in underwear or loose, light colored cotton clothing. Begin by rubbing your hands briskly together for about one minute in order to fully sensitize them. Then, starting as high above the crown as you can reach, methodically run your hands through the client's auric field, about five inches from the body. Slowly work your way from the crown to the feet, tracing the contours of all sides of the body.

Auric holes will feel either cooler or warmer than the rest of the aura — sometimes they feel tingly. If you find an area that feels like a hole, put your left hand over it, close your eyes, visualize the aura as pure luminous white light, and see if the suspicious area looks dark to your inner vision. Work slowly and carefully: if your hands lose their sensitivity, rub them briskly together again.

4. Guessing: Sometimes it is fairly easy to guess where holes might be, although it is preferable to use one of the above methods whenever possible. With drugs, alcohol, and tobacco, holes are likely to accumulate in the crown energy, third eye region, throat and chest. In the case of illness or injury, holes are generally found over the affected part of the body. Air pollution and pesticides primarily affect the throat and lungs; food additives affect the gastro-intestinal tract; loud noise affects the crown, ears and solar plexus; negative emotions affect the crown, third eye, throat, heart and solar plexus. Negative entities usually lodge in the chakras about one to three inches out from the body, or hide in the back of the aura.

Using The Light Weaver

After probable holes are located, they can generally be easily patched. If you suspect the presence of negative entities (characterized by addictions, nightmares, erratic behavior, hallucinations, offensive voices, the inability to distinguish reality from unpleasant fantasies and so on) the Michael Power Tool should be used first on every chakra and hole in order to remove the entities.

Assuming the chakras are clear, begin by holding your Light Weaver Disk in your left hand (or in your right hand if you are left-handed.) Hold it by the edges with your thumb and index finger, so your hand is not covering the face of the disk. The weave pattern should be held so the lines run horizontally and vertically. Locate the auric hole, and place the disk over the hole right up against the client's body.

Next, use the palm of your right hand or your bunched fingers to project energy through the disk: visualize that as the energy flows through the disk it takes on the disk's interlacing pattern and begins to fill the hole with tightly woven strands of lilac light. A strobe light or a clear quartz crystal may also be used to project energy through the disk. If you use a strobe light, *please remember to never, ever, strobe a person with epilepsy.*

As you project energy through the Light Weaver, slowly pull the disk away from the body straight out through the auric field, visualizing that the weaving is extending outward. Basically you are filling the auric hole with a plug of woven energy.

Repeat this process 3 times for every hole, rotating the disk about 15 degrees each time for a diagonal weave. Visualize that each reweave is filling the hole in more and more solidly. Then recheck the aura visually or with your hands to see if any holes remain. When all the holes are filled, move your hand or crystal through the patched areas in a circular, polishing motion to smooth the aura out and fill in any small gaps.

After a week or two recheck the aura, especially if the damage was heavy. With severe or chronic cases you may use your Light Weaver Disk to fill or refill holes as often as necessary.

Professional healers will find that simply strobing the Light Weaver for a minute or two on each client's heart chakra at the beginning of a session will fortify the aura to the extent that your other healing work will be much more effective and last longer.

If you have no one to use the light weaver on your own body, you may place the disk on your heart chakra and strobe it for one or two minutes. This will put a quick patch throughout your entire auric field.

4

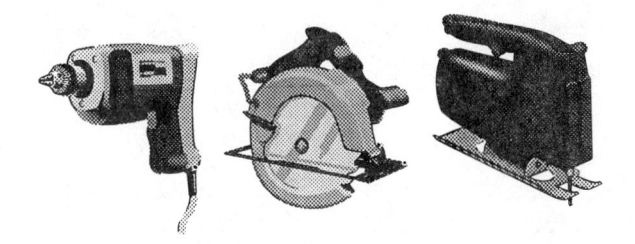

The Grounding Disk

The Grounding Power Tool is the simplest disk to use, but its potential is vast.

Many lightworkers mistakenly confuse "grounding" with "earthbound." They do not wish to be grounded because they feel they will lose whatever tenuous meditative connection they have with the finer planes. This connection is usually perceived as a general spaciness, such as you might feel after drinking a glass of beer or wine, and involves a pleasant, unfocused, hazy state of mind. If you are burdened with difficulties in your personal or work life, this sensation can be a mild respite from worry and preoccupation.

However, if you wish to achieve the deep states of concentration and meditation that lead to healing, channeling, contact with Angels and Masters, past life recall, inner transformation, and self-realization, you must be grounded. *Grounding turns your entire body into an antenna which receives incoming psychic impressions and information through the crown chakra, and anchors them down into the physical brain where you can explore them, remember them, and use them in your physical life.* This means you will not experience that spacey feeling that leaves you staring at walls with no memory of what you are vaguely sensing: instead you will ground your central nervous system so it can experience the crystal-clear enlightenment that precedes, and is part of, the bliss state. And when the experience is over, you will have excellent recall of what you have seen and felt.

The Grounding Disk literally *plugs you in*, putting high-level experiences well within your reach — especially when used in conjunction with other Power Tools, and most especially with the Inner Eye Disk.

Using The Grounding Disk

The Grounding Power Tool is always used on the lower part of the body. During a healing session the disk is normally placed directly on the front of the body at the first chakra (right over the pubic region.) If bulky clothing makes it difficult to balance the disk over the first chakra, it may be placed between the legs or below the feet.

If you lie down during meditation, the Grounding Disk should be placed on the first chakra if possible. If you sit for meditation, the disk may be placed between your legs, on your lap, or in your left pants pocket.

The Grounding Disk should remain in place during the entire healing or meditation session: early removal will break your psychic connection and leave you floating in space.

After an Intense Session

Frequently after a profound healing or meditation session when no grounding device is used, a person is left with a great deal of high-vibrational energy circulating through his physical and subtle bodies, and as he comes out of his state of deep concentration he has difficulty focusing on the physical level. When this happens to you or a client, simply hold the Grounding Disk in the left hand and sit quietly for a few minutes, breathing deeply through the solar plexus until the mind is clear and tranquil.

Other Situations

Any time a person has undergone intense emotional upset such as deep anger, numbing grief, a sudden shock, an unpleasant surprise, and so on, the Grounding Disk may be used as above, held in the left hand while breathing deeply and slowly through the solar plexus. If the situation is extreme, the disk may be carried in the left pants pocket for an hour or two until a calm mental and emotional state is achieved.

Everyone Should Have One

As you can see, the Grounding Disk delivers a great deal of benefit for very little effort. If you meditate, channel, and/or heal, this disk will significantly improve your personal efforts and the results experienced by your clients.

5

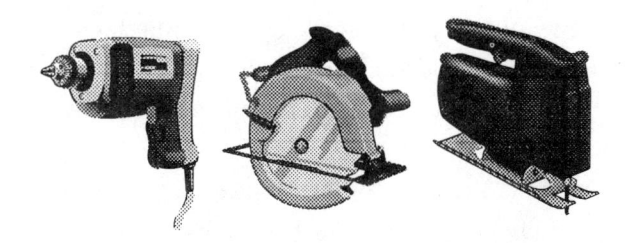

The Magnet Disk

Healers from all over the world report finding bizarre astral devices in their client's auras. Removing these objects proves difficult and time-consuming. The Magnet Power Tool uses astral magnetism and purifying blue light to easily pull such artifacts out of the auric field and destroy them on contact.

Auric Implants

Auric implants are really nothing more than holographic thought forms of varying intensity, origin and purpose. We are all exposed to vast numbers of thought forms every day because the earth's psychic atmosphere is every bit as polluted as its physical atmosphere, and probably much, much more so: rolling through psychic space are huge noxious clouds of twisted and distorted thoughts created by terror, anxiety, grief, and depression, as well as by severe mental and emotional imbalance. These thought forms can attach themselves to a person's auric field, causing many symptoms that are difficult to diagnose. We will discuss five types of thought forms that cause special problems.

1. Astral parasites: Frequently when a person is weakened through drug, tobacco, or alcohol abuse, personal difficulty, illness, or injury, he or she is susceptible to astral parasites which enter an unstable auric field and lodge there in order to feed on life force. These creatures are sometimes mistaken for auric implants, although in reality they are simply opportunistic low-vibrational elementals that have found a comfortable home. A common example would be the plethora of muddy red leech-like creatures that infest many auras.

2. Personal thought forms: A second group of objects found in auric fields is actually produced by the afflicted person himself. This type of thought form turns back and works against its creator. Sometimes this is a simple case of karma returning; other times it is a form of self-punishment for some real or imagined transgression or fault. Example: a little hammer-like object that bashes a person in the head every time he has what he considers to be an improper thought.

3. Remnants of past lives: One of the most common sights in the aura is debris from past lives. For example, if a man was killed in a pioneer lifetime by a hatchet blow to the abdomen, a person with inner vision might still see the astral image of a metal axehead buried in the victim's aura over the solar plexus.

4. True implants: A fourth type of auric implant is exactly what the name implies: a device that has been purposely planted in a person's aura by someone else. These can be positive, for healing purposes, or negative. Power Tools are a perfect example of a positive implant which puts a holographic image into a person's aura, where it acts as a time-release capsule emanating healing vibrations over a period of several weeks. Negative implants, however, are the work of black magicians; they invariably try to harm their victim or drain them of vital life force. These implants take many distorted, grotesque forms — a bloody, jagged knife in the back or some sort of weird torturous mechanical device would be typical.

5. Holographic information: It should be clearly understood that not every holographic object found in an aura is negative. All of us have many little thought forms in our auras that relate to our past and present lives: faces of loved ones, plans for projects, tools of our trade, spiritual symbols, and the like. The Magnet Disk will leave these objects in place, focusing only on holographic items that have a distinctly negative, harmful vibration.

Finding Implants

Auric implants of a negative nature may be located in four ways: by looking at the auric field; through meditation; by "feeling" the aura; or by an educated guess. Implant finding is best accomplished by someone other than the person with the suspected problem, since implants can distort perception of oneself. Whichever method you use, listen carefully to your inner guidance. You will note that these procedures are the same as those given for finding auric holes in the instructions for the Lightweaver Disk.

1. Looking at the aura: If you can see auras, you have an enormous advantage. Begin by standing the client in front of a white or black background, whichever is best for your auric vision. The aura is best seen when the body is naked — if this is not possible, underwear or loose, light-colored cotton clothing will do.

Some people find it easier to see the aura with their eyes half closed, or slightly out of focus, or by looking out of the corner of their eyes.

Stand 8-10 feet from your client and scan from about 24 inches above the head down below the feet. Begin with the front of the aura, then have the client slowly turn 360 degrees. Check the back of the aura very carefully.

2. Scanning the aura in meditation: Sit in a comfortable position 8-10 feet away from the client, who should be dressed as described above. Holding the Inner Eye Power Tool up to your forehead for three to four minutes before beginning will help boost your ability to detect implants.

Start with the client facing you: close your eyes and visualize a glowing white light surrounding her/him. As above, scan from the crown energy down to the feet, having the client slowly rotate 360 degrees. The difference is that in this case your eyes are closed and you are relying on your inner vision to show you objects in the aura. Any implant of a negative nature should appear to your psychic sight as a dark, ominous structure against the clear light of the auric field.

3. Feeling the aura: With a little practice the aura is surprisingly easy to feel. As always for auric work the client should be naked or dressed in underwear or loose, light colored cotton clothing. Begin by rubbing your hands briskly together for about one minute in order to fully sensitize them. Then, starting as high above the crown as you can reach, methodically run your hands through he client's auric field about five inches from the body. Slowly work your way down from the crown chakra, tracing the contours of all sides of the body all the way down to the feet. It is important to scan near the feet because remnants of past lives are often found in this area.

Implants feel either cooler or warmer than the rest of the aura — they can also feel tingly or sharp or unpleasant. If you find an area that feels like an implant, put your left hand over it, close your eyes, visualize the aura as pure luminous white light, and see if the suspicious area looks dark to your inner vision. Work slowly and carefully: if you hands lose their sensitivity, rub them briskly together again until you work up more heat.

4. Guessing: Sometimes it is fairly easy to guess where implants might be, although it is preferable to use one of the above methods whenever possible. If drugs, alcohol or tobacco have been used habitually it is safe to assume that implants, negative thought forms, negative entities, and holes are likely to accumulate in any or all of the chakras from one to five inches out from the body, in both the front and back. In the case of illness or injury, auric problems are generally found over the affected part of the body. Past life remnants are frequently found over sites of chronic problems, as well as below the knees and down around the feet.

Using the Magnet Disk

When you find a suspected implant simply place the Magnet Disk in the auric field right in the middle of the implant and strobe the disk for two minutes. The Power Tool will magnetize the implant, pull it into the disk, and disintegrate it.

If you suspect implants but cannot find them, try strobing the Magnet Disk in a straight line down both the front and the back of the chakras from about five inches away, starting at the crown and working your way to the feet.

In routine healing if you are pressed for time or using other Power Tools as your primary focus, the Magnet Disk may be placed on the heart chakra and strobed for one minute simply as a precautionary measure, then left in place while you carry out your other healing chores.

Finishing Up

After the session be sure to clean your Magnet Disk thoroughly, as it will likely be filled with obnoxious debris from any implants that it has located and destroyed. Be sure to wash your hands and forearms thoroughly also, for the same reason.

Companion Disks

If you do a lot of auric work, you will find that the Magnet Disk is particularly useful when combined with several other Power Tools. The Michael Disk specializes in removing astral parasites, foul entities, and unpleasant elementals from the aura, and offers protection against black magicians; the Exterminator focuses on negative thought forms of a general, global nature; and the Light Weaver will quickly and easily repair auric holes after negative entities, thought forms and implants have been removed.

6

The Pink Rose Disk

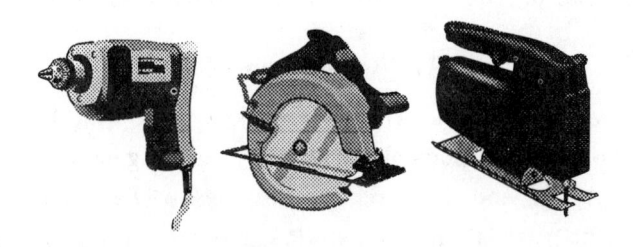

The Pink Rose Disk is for healing present or past life trauma related to violent, unfulfilled, or unhappy relationships, and for opening the mind, heart and soul in such a way that they can experience and radiate true spiritual love. The Pink Rose also excels in clearing, purifying, tuning, and energizing the heart and crown chakras. When the heart and crown chakras are balanced, and suppressed negative energies are cleared, tension and emotional extremes are released. The result is inner tranquility and the ability to radiate unhesitating, undistorted divine love.

It is reasonable to assume that virtually everyone on Earth has suffered from frustrating and/or harmful relationships during several — and probably many — incarnations. Because past life trauma is stored in the DNA, we tend to be largely unaware of the full scope of its devastating effects. However, if you could focus your consciousness down to the molecular level, you would feel searing pain in the segments of DNA that have been damaged by traumatic relationships. Furthermore, of all the various types of trauma, love trauma is among the most agonizing due to the emotional, mental, spiritual, and often physical anguish that it produces.

The great angelic blessing within the Pink Rose Disk is that it resolves and heals love wounds carried in the DNA. The disk's gentle, soothing, uplifting effect allows this old trauma to be released so proper healing can occur from the DNA molecules on up.

Angels, Flowers, and Gems

All members of the Angelic Kingdom work with divine energy. Some are responsible for modifying the genetic codes of flowers, herbs, and trees; others create growth and vibrational patterns for crystals and gems; while still others work with Earth's vital grid system of high-energy vortices and ley lines.

A large number of Angels specialize in using the divine energies of plants and gems for healing. Many of these healing Angels work in voluntary cooperation with human healers in order to further humanity's physical and spiritual well-being, growth, and understanding.

Some of the outstanding characteristics of the nature Power Tools are their rich colors, their kaleidoscopic patterns, and the beautiful angelic combinations of flowers, gems and other types of natural flora and fauna.

Power Tools carry the very highest vibrations of the plants and gems portrayed on them. This high-vibrational energy is transferred into each disk through the medium of light, which picks up the imprint of a plant or gem's spiritual energy pattern (*the signature*).

The Elements of the Disk

The Pink Rose Disk reproduces the energy signatures of the pink rose and two gemstones.

Pink Rose is symbolic of constantly unfolding Divine Love. Here is an absolute, unconditional love that nothing can change or harm: it lasts forever, maintaining its freshness and purity throughout all of eternity. This is a great, dazzling love, in all of its myriad manifestations, including the mystical love between the Creator and the created; the tender relationship between lovers; the unconditional bonds between parent and child or between siblings; and the honest, open love between friends. It also includes the love of nature, of plants and animals, of the Earth, and of life itself.

Ruby is the master heart gem. It balances, purifies, and stabilizes the heart chakra and the physical heart, causing energy to radiate out from the heart center. Ruby calls forth divine, unselfish devotion, courage, and sacrifice. It also clears negative thoughts and promotes stability, confidence, tranquility, and self-esteem, while easing grief, disappointment, melancholy, anger, and depression. Ruby is excellent for depleted vitality.

Diamond alleviates negative patterns and intensifies life force. It is good for anxiety, insecurity, low self-esteem, envy, jealousy, tension, and stress — all of which can result from unhappy love relationships. Diamond brings radiant white light through the crown and/or heart chakra into the system of physical and subtle bodies. For further information regarding the physical properties of gemstones, consult with *Gem Elixirs and Vibrational Healing, Vol. 1*, by Gurudas.

Using the Pink Rose Disk

Because of its particular combination of plants and gems, the Rose Disk is used on the heart chakra and above the crown. From either position the disk's healing energy will spread throughout the entire system. If the disk is to be used to heal emotional scars, place it on the heart chakra; if it is to be used to heal psychological scars, place it above the crown. During a deep healing session it is advantageous to use it on both chakras.

The Pink Rose Disk is "dialed" or rotated so different gems are in direct alignment with the spinal energies. This allows you to select which gemstones are dominant at any given time.

For general purposes, begin by placing the disk above the crown chakra and dialing it so the diamonds are north-south-east-west in relation to the spine: this placement selects the diamond energies as the primary gem vibration. Strobe the disk for two minutes in this position. Then place the disk on the heart chakra and rotate it so the rubies are north-south-east-west. Now the rubies are primary, and their energies will be predominant: strobe the disk for another two minutes in this position. (Since it occupies the center of the disk, the rose energy always has a primary role.) If you are working by room light, use the disk for ten to twenty minutes in each position.

The first gem position removes negative patterns and blocks, flooding the system with white light; the second position finishes disintegrating negativity and sends divine love flowing out through the heart chakra.

Tracking Down Problems

Any thoughts, psychic perceptions, or old issues which surface during the session should be carefully examined. If you do past life regressions, it is extremely helpful to try to determine the *cause and circumstances* of past trauma so it can be thoroughly understood and therefore more fully released. Depending on how you work, the disk may be used before, during, or after the regression. Be sure to look for more than one trauma: most people have many instances of deep love-related trauma from their present as well as their past lives. It could take several sessions to find the roots and patterns of all the major problems, but the ensuing deep healing and the release of pain and stress will more than repay you for your efforts.

Tracking down trauma is best done with the Inner Eye Power Tool on the forehead, the Pink Rose over the heart, the Rainbow Disk at the solar plexus, and the Grounding Disk at the first chakra. If a full past life regression cannot be done, the following technique will be useful to both the client and the healer. During or after the strobing of the disk, visualize that you are walking into a movie theater, sitting down, and looking at the blank movie screen. Watch for scenes of past life trauma to appear on the screen as they surface from the damaged DNA. If the client is more clairaudient than clairvoyant, he or she can visualize a radio instead of a movie, and listen to a news broadcast describing the past traumatic events.

Any further information which is needed regarding old trauma will usually surface at night, generally in the form of troubling dreams or nightmares. These should be carefully recorded and analyzed.

Meditation Technique

After clearing trauma, the following meditation will help open the heart chakra to receive incoming spiritual light. Visualize that your heart chakra is a luminous pink rosebud, and then imagine that the bud is beginning to unfold. Picture the outer layer of petals falling open, then the next layer, the next, and so on. When the rose is fully opened, visualize that it is flooded with pink and gold light, causing the rose to increase in size until it fills the whole room . . . the planet . . . the universe.

If you would like to send love to someone in particular, visualize the rosebud opening right over that person's heart chakra . . . expanding . . . and filling their whole body with pink and gold light.

7

The Red Poppy Disk

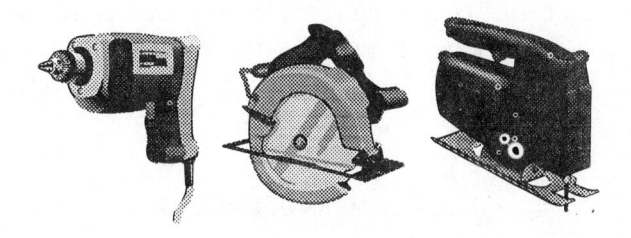

The Red Poppy Disk clears, tunes, and energizes the first (base) chakra; releases the current and past life stress which accumulates in this chakra; and raises the kundalini life force. When first chakra tension is released, it is easier to maintain inner balance.

Much of the stress stored in the first chakra is of a sexual nature: the Angels tell us that virtually everyone on Earth has suffered sexual trauma during several — and probably many — incarnations. Because past life trauma is stored in the DNA, we tend to be largely unaware of it. However, those who are able to focus their consciousness down to the molecular level report a feeling of searing agony in the segments of DNA that have been maimed by sexual trauma. Furthermore, of all the various types of trauma, sexual trauma is just about the worst, due to the extreme physical, emotional, mental and physical anguish that it produces.

The great angelic blessing of the Red Poppy Disk is that it numbs pain stored in the DNA — specifically sexual distress — allowing the body to relax at the molecular level. This soothing, unclenching effect allows old trauma to be released so proper healing can occur from the DNA molecules on up. Because it numbs unbearable sexual pain on so many vital levels, the Angels refer to the Red Poppy as *the merciful disk.*

Many professional healers work with this disk, and they have a large number of clients who have experienced profound relief after a session with the Red Poppy. Healers should also use this disk on themselves in order to understand the profound depths at which it works.

The Elements of the Disk

The Red Poppy Disk reproduces the energy signatures of one flower and four gems. The black background supplies the grounding which is necessary while this particular flower and crystal combination does its work.

Red Poppy is a narcotic, as are all members of the poppy family. The red poppy's sacred energy signature desensitizes, numbs, and sedates trauma-damaged DNA. The pure red color of the poppy is deeply healing and energizing.

Smoky Quartz produces an ultra-sound frequency that disintegrates trauma released by the DNA; purifies the lower chakras; stimulates the first chakra so it becomes radiant with light; channels white light from the crown chakra and love from the heart chakra down into the first chakra; initiates the kundalini flow; is a sedative and a relaxant.

Clear Quartz combined with smoky quartz creates a tremendous balancing, healing, and cleansing; clears and neutralizes negativity; heals the emotions; reintegrates levels of consciousness; and alleviates emotional extremes, especially hysteria.

Amethyst purifies and amplifies life energies; changes molecular structure; eases anxieties; and also produces an ultra-sound frequency that disintegrates trauma released by the DNA. Amethyst is the energy of spiritual transmutation.

Emerald stabilizes the astral (emotional) body; alleviates hidden fears; brings physical, mental, and emotional equilibrium and tranquility; draws wisdom and divine love from the spiritual planes; decrystallizes old patterns; initiates deep healing and regeneration; and prepares body and soul for spiritual advancement.

The source for these crystal attribute is *Gem Elixirs and Vibrational Healing, Vol. 1* by Gurudas.

Using the Poppy Disk

Because of the black background which grounds physical energy, the Red Poppy Disk is *always* used on the first chakra. From this position its healing energy is spread throughout the entire chakra system as the kundalini flows up the spine, carrying the disk's energy signatures with it.

You may use the disk on either the front of the first chakra (the pubic area) or on the back of the chakra, right over the coccyx. Unless there is spinal damage, the disk is generally used on the front of the body.

Mandala Power Tools are "dialed" or rotated so different gems or combinations of gems are in direct alignment with the spinal energies. This allows you to select which gemstones are dominant at any given time.

For general purposes, begin by dialing the disk so the emerald/smoky quartz combination is north-south-east-west in relation to the spine. This placement selects the emerald/smoky energies as the primary gem vibrations. Strobe the disk for two minutes in this position. Then rotate the disk so the amethyst/clear quartz combination is north-south-east-west. Now this gem combination is primary, and its energies will be predominant: strobe the disk for another two minutes in this position. If you are working by room light, use the disk for ten to twenty minutes in each position.

The emerald/smoky gem combination breaks up the worst of

the trauma and soothes molecular pain, while the amethyst/clear quartz combination finishes disintegrating the trauma and pulls in purifying white light. Both combinations initiate deep healing, reenergize the chakra, and flood it with spiritual energy.

Finding Trauma

Any thoughts, psychic perceptions, or old issues which surface during the session should be carefully examined. *If you do past life regressions, it is extremely helpful to try to determine the cause and circumstances of past trauma so it can be thoroughly understood and therefore more fully released.* Depending on how you work, the disk may be used before, during, or after the regression. Be sure to look for more than one trauma: most people have many instances of sexual trauma from their present as well as their past lives. It could take several sessions to find the roots and patterns of all the major problems, but the ensuing deep healing and the release of pain and stress will more than repay you for your efforts. As mentioned earlier, if you do not do past life work, the Angel Academy book *Light from the Angels* will show you several ways to read past lives and find old trauma.

As with the Pink Rose disk, if a past life regression cannot be done the following technique will be useful to both the client and the healer. During or after the strobing of the disk, visualize that you are walking into a movie theater, sitting down, and looking at the blank movie screen. Watch for scenes of past life trauma to appear on the screen as they surface from the damaged DNA. If the client is more clairaudient than clairvoyant, he or she can visualize a radio instead of a movie, and listen to a news broadcast describing the past traumatic events.

Tracking down trauma is best done with the Inner Eye Power Tool on the forehead, the Pink Rose over the heart, the Rainbow Disk at the solar plexus, and the Red Poppy on the first chakra.

Putting the Puzzle Together

Any further information which is needed regarding old trauma will usually surface at night, usually in the form of troubling dreams or nightmares. These should be carefully recorded and analyzed because they generally carry fragments of information being released from the DNA.

If the trauma is especially deep or if there are several instances of trauma, it is a good idea to use the Red Poppy once every three or four weeks until no more trauma surfaces.

After using the Red Poppy the recipient of the disk's energy is likely to be somewhat subdued, contemplative, and preoccupied as he or she processes the knowledge that has been gained through the session. But after two or three days this condition should alleviate totally, changing into a state of deep physical relaxation accompanied by profound spiritual, emotional and mental relief.

8

The Exterminator

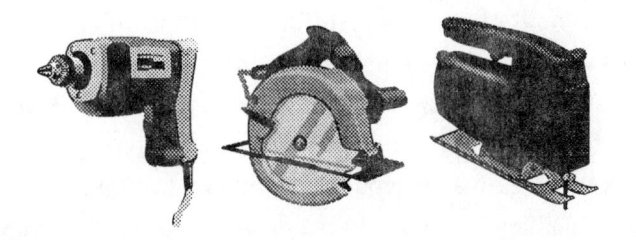

The Exterminator Power Tool specializes in destroying negative thought forms and negative perceptions.

The Spiritual Masters tell us that negative thought forms caused by planetary war, violence, disease, starvation and the like are constantly circulating the Earth, permeating every part of our psychic atmosphere. Because they are formed by strongly disruptive forces such as violence, fear, and misery, negative thought forms have considerable energy behind them and can linger for thousands of years.

All of these past and present negative energies are constantly flowing like dark clouds into our homes, where they have the potential to interfere with our inner tranquility and disturb our meditations and sleep. Furthermore, healers find that their healing rooms quickly fill up with additional trauma released by their clients. Many lightworkers use smudge or incense to clear their homes or healing rooms of these cumulative negative vibrations, but the Masters inform us that once a room is cleared it will refill with negative vibrations within fifteen minutes if you live in a city and within a day if you live in the country.

The first great blessing of the Exterminator Disk is that it destroys negative thought forms the moment they enter your home or healing room, giving you a permanent atmosphere of high spiritual energy and light.

The second great blessing of the Exterminator Disk is that it destroys the negative thought forms which are the nucleus of disease states. This means that the Exterminator literally pulls the rug out from under physical, mental and emotional problems by clearing the negative perceptions and thought forms that produce disease, tension, agitation, depression and emotional extremes.

As the Exterminator blitzes negativity, proper healing can occur from the DNA molecules on up. The result is deep-seated physical, emotional, mental and spiritual equilibrium. This makes it possible for healers to produce more permanent results, taking the first step toward putting an end to chronic problems.

As always, the healer must take into consideration the fact that disease serves the function of teaching lessons and repaying karma, and that many diseases will not be ready to be released until the lesson is learned and/or the karma repaid. However, if a problem is due to be released in this lifetime, the Exterminator will begin the process quickly and efficiently.

The Elements of the Disk

The Exterminator Disk reproduces the energy signatures of five plants and one gem. All five of the plants are notorious for destroying harmful organisms on the physical level, while on the spiritual level they destroy a broad spectrum of negative thought forms, which are the astral equivalents of dangerous insects, parasites and viruses. Just as parasitic physical entities debilitate the host's physical energy, so negative thought forms (*elementals*) pull life force from their host's astral body, which leads to physical weakness and disease.

The five exterminator plants on the disk are the **fly agaric mushroom, rue, pennyroyal, garlic and wormwood**. The fly agaric not only destroys negativity, but it also has the additional quality of bringing a vibration of cosmic consciousness into your meditations, which helps you see the negativity that is affecting you and allows you to trace its origins.

The **brown tourmaline** gemstone in the center of the disk destroys very heavy-duty negative vibrations, giving the disk a full spectrum of protective vibrations.

Clearing with the Disk

To clear a room or house with the Exterminator, simply place it in a location that receives plenty of indirect lighting. If you have a light box, the disk may be used on it, but the box should only have the light on for a maximum of sixty minutes a day. Remember, the Exterminator is a powerful disk, and too much light over an extended period of time will rev it up to the point where it begins to erode your etheric body.

Healing with the Disk

During a healing session the Exterminator is used primarily at the crown, third eye, heart, throat, and solar plexus chakras. To clear negative thought forms at the mental level, place the disk above the head in the crown energy, the third eye, or the throat. To clear negativity at the astral/emotional level, place the disk on the throat, heart, or solar plexus. To clear negative thought forms on the spiritual and physical levels, place the disk at the crown, third eye, throat, or on the heart chakra. If time permits, it is best to use the disk on all five upper chakras for a complete clearing at all levels.

If you are dealing with a specific problem area, the disk may also be placed there. For a very thorough removal of negativity, use the disk on every main chakra front and back, starting at the base chakra and working up to the crown.

If room light is used, the disk should be kept on each chakra for ten minutes. If a strobe is used, strobe the disk for a maximum of two minutes per chakra. After strobing, the disk may be left in place on the heart and/or solar plexus for another ten minutes or so during the meditation exercise (see below), and then moved up into the crown chakra where it can remain for the rest of the session.

The Exterminator is "dialed" or rotated so different plants or gems are in direct alignment with the spinal energies. This allows you to choose which vibrations are dominant at any given time.

When you first place the Exterminator Disk on a chakra, rotate it so the mushrooms are in a north-south, east-west position relative to the head. After strobing for one minute (or five minutes of room light), rotate the disk so the garlic-rue-pennyroyal combination is in the north-south-east-west position. The wormwood and tourmaline are always active in a primary role, since they are in the center of the disk.

While the disk is in each position, the following meditation technique should be used to scan for the specific negativities that the disk is clearing.

Meditation Technique

Visualize that you are looking through a brightly lit microscope for astral insects, parasites, viruses and the like (nucleus negative thought forms.) When you find something, ask your guides to identify it for you, show you its origin in your life, how it affects you, and what purpose it has served. Then watch as the Exterminator vaporizes it.

As always, deep meditation is greatly facilitated by using the Exterminator in conjunction with the Inner Eye Disk, the Grounding Disk, and any other Power Tool your inner guidance suggests.

Tracing Origins

Any thoughts, psychic perceptions or old issues which surface during the meditation should be carefully examined. If you do current and past life regressions, it is extremely helpful to try to find both the original nucleus and subsequent ramifications of negative thoughts, emotions or perceptions for each problem, so it can be thoroughly understood and therefore more fully released. Such conditions generally begin in one specific incarnation and then gather strength throughout successive incarnations. Also, be sure to look for more than one nucleus of negativity: most people have dozens of tangled, interrelated negative perceptions that require deep-level unraveling before they can be examined and cleared. It could take several sessions to find the origins and patterns of major problems, but it is definitely worth the time and trouble to do so.

Any further information which is needed regarding old trauma will probably either appear in your meditations or surface at night, generally in the form of troubling dreams or nightmares. These are signs that the disk has done its work; what you see in meditation or disturbing dreams is negativity that the Exterminator has uncovered. This additional information should be carefully recorded and analyzed, as it will show you profound connections that you probably never knew existed between past occurrences and present difficulties.

9

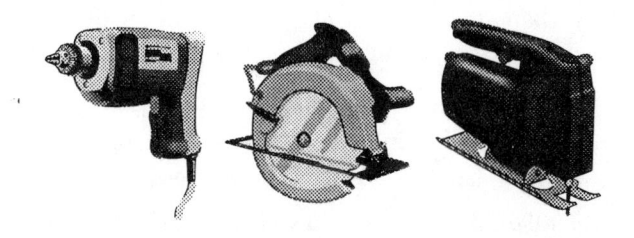

The Michael Disk

The Michael Disk is an astral portrait of the Archangel Michael: it acts as a channeling window for Michael, who sends his energy through the disk in huge quantities.

On the disk is an accurate portrait of Michael as he appears when he descends into the lower astral levels to combat negative entities, which he does in order to serve and protect humanity. His inner aura of white light protects him from the lower astral vibrational field, while his outer aura flashes out behind him like blue flames. The sword cuts psychic ties, and the small scale at his waist is symbolic of Michael's authority to return karma to negative entities.

Use the Michael Disk for extreme cases of mental and emotional imbalance stemming from suspected possession; for warding off psychic attack; for cutting psychic ties; for addictions of all types; with people in very possessive relationships; with people who feel violent urges which go against their nature; with people who hear unpleasant voices; and with people who work in hospitals, clinics, bars and other sites of suffering and accumulated negative thought forms.

Types Of Negativity

Possessing entities are low-level astral tramps, thugs, bullies and freeloaders who attempt to control a person's mind and body, influencing them toward destructive behavior which often includes alcohol, drugs, and violent sexual activities. Normally we are well defended against such entities, but in times of trauma, stress, substance abuse, injury, or illness, our protective auric shield forms holes which are slow to heal. Whenever one or more degraded astral entities find such a weakness in an aura, they enter and embed themselves in the victim's energy field.

Negative thought forms are caused by negative thinking, negative feelings, and negative habits. With repetition, these thoughts acquire life force and become low vibrational parasitic entities (*elementals*) which lodge in the chakras, influencing a person to do things he would not normally do.

Possessing entities, negative elementals and negative thought forms are like leeches which absorb vital force as it flows through the aura and the chakras on its way into the body.

Chakras are normally protected by an etheric web, which stretches like a drum head between the body and the front of each chakra. This web filters out harmful energies and keeps them from entering the body through the auric field. However, as mentioned above, strong negative emotions such as anger, fear or depression rip this protective web, providing negative elementals with an easy lodging place. Drugs, alcohol and tobacco also rupture the protective web and attract negative entities.

Psychic Ties

Psychic ties are astral cords which are sent out by one person to wrap around another person's chakras. These ties interfere with the second person's will power, and tend to cause him to act as the first person wishes.

Frequently such ties are put out unintentionally by a friend, spouse or relative who is trying to convince the other person to take a particular action. On rarer occasions ties can be sent out by black magicians in order to force another person to obey harmful psychic commands — the heavy use of drugs or alcohol is almost always involved in this instance.

Using the Disk

White cotton clothing that does not inhibit the auric field is best for a session with the Michael Disk. Avoid belts, bras, jewelry and shoes.

Before and after using the disk on others, the healer should use the Michael Disk on her/himself in order to clear negative ties and elementals picked up from clients.

When working with the Michael Disk it is easiest for the client to sit on a small stool. The disk is held on the first chakra on the front of the body, then moved to the back of the chakra on the spine. When the base chakra is cleared, move up to the second chakra, then the navel, and so on, up to and including the crown chakra. Clear each chakra front and back, then place the disk over each ear.

A strobe light is by far the most powerful way to use the Michael Disk. The strobe is used on each chakra for one minute front and back for simple problems, or two minutes for severe cases. However, please remember to *never, ever, strobe a person with epilepsy.*

If you don't have a strobe, allow five minutes per chakra for simple problems, and up to twenty minutes per chakra for severe cases where possession, drugs, or alcohol ar suspected. As negative elementals are detached, unpleasant odors may be released from the aura.

While you work, mentally (or using a pendulum) rescan the chakras and auric field to be certain no elementals or ties remain. The person being worked on can also scan inwardly — the Inner Eye Disk and the Grounding Disk will make this easier. When you are finished, visualize great waves of icy blue-white light spiraling up from the client's feet and down from his crown, dissolving any lingering debris.

You will find that ties are cut very quickly and cleanly, parasitic entities are removed, and auric holes are filled with light and begin to mend. To complete the repair, use the Light Weaver Disk.

After using the Michael Disk you might wish to reenergize the affected chakras with other Power Tools, or with your hands, crystals, a light wand, pendulum, etc.

When you are finished, be sure to clean your hands, disks, and healing room well. If at all possible, after cleaning the Michael Disk use it again on yourself to clear any parasitic entities or ties that might have jumped ship from your client's auric field into your own.

After the Session

A client is liable to have strange dreams for several days after a session with the Michael Disk. Usually these dreams are quite unpleasant due to the fact that they show the entities that have been encountered, and these entities tend to manifest as sucking or poisonous creatures such as insects, leeches, toads, bats and snakes. However, such dreams are actually quite positive, indicating that the negativity has lost its camouflage ability and has been cleared from the auric field.

If possible, after a week or ten days rescan the aura to be certain that it is clear. If any problem areas remain, repeat the above process.

After ties and negative entities are removed, many positive changes should occur as your client begins to receive large quantities of energy that are no longer being absorbed by parasitic entities. He or she is likely to have more physical energy and to be able to go deeper into the meditative state, while any compulsions, destructive tendencies, violent inner voices or physical symptoms that might have been present should disappear.

Specific Problems

The following list will give a general idea as to which chakras are usually involved with particular ailments. Although every chakra should be cleared during a session, the indicated chakras should be examined with special care, as they are generally trouble areas.

Stress: Clear the front and back solar plexus, third eye, and crown chakras.

Suspected past life trauma: Clear the solar plexus front and back, third eye, and crown. Scan the astral body (especially the base and second chakras) for the sites of old past life injuries and clear these areas also.

Compulsive eating: The front and back solar plexus chakras are likely to be cracked and have negative elementals; the throat chakra is also affected.

Smoking: Smoke elementals (appearing as small muddy red/orange flames) and cracks accumulate in the throat chakra. Negative elementals are also found at the front and back solar plexus, third eye, and crown.

Alcohol: Large desire elementals which take the form of leeches are deeply embedded in the front and back solar plexus and throat. Other negative elementals are at the third eye and crown.

Drug Addition: Cracks, punctures, holes, and very large leech-like desire elementals are found in the front and back solar plexus, throat, third eye and crown chakras. Carefully check the base and second chakras also.

For further information on elementals in the chakras refer to

Choa Kok Sui's beautiful book on *Pranic Healing*.

Meet Michael

If you wish to connect with Michael and his band of Protective Angels in a more personal way, sit gazing at the disk in a well-lit room. Then put the disk above your crown chakra or on your heart and watch for Michael to appear. His energy is very pure and very sweet. If you have difficulty meditating, use the Inner Eye Disk and the Grounding Disk, combined with the Master Meditation Technique given with the Inner Eye information.

10

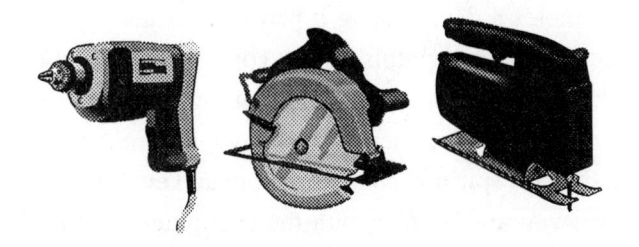

The Isis Disk

Isis is one of the most revered forms of the Divine Mother ever to appear to mankind. The ancient Egyptians called her "The Great Goddess," "The Mother of the Gods," and "The Living One." She is a goddess of immense psychic, metaphysical and spiritual power. In Egyptian art, Isis is commonly represented as a protective deity with her wings outstretched around the devotee. The wings indicate that she is from the Angelic Kingdom.

Isis exists . . . she is a very real higher-dimensional Angelic Guardian who has watched lovingly over the Earth for eons. If you feel you were incarnate in dynastic Egypt, you will probably find that Isis holds special meaning for you. If you were an Initiate in one of the Isis Temples, you can be certain that she has touched your heart in a poignant, profound way.

The Isis Power Tool is an astral portrait which has been channeled from Isis herself: every detail is authentic. The disk is a way to raise your consciousness; a way to reestablish contact with Isis; a way to renew ancient vows; a way to reenter into a state of divine grace; and a way to receive divine inspiration and spiritual nourishment.

Establishing Contact with Isis

It is relatively easy to establish contact with Isis through the medium of the disk. Begin by handling it regularly for about fifteen minutes a day, making it part of your daily routine. Isis' vibration flows through this Power Tool in huge quantities, so as you handle the disk her energy is pouring into your auric field, mixing with your own energy, raising your vibrations, and acting as a catalyst for spiritual change, growth and evolution.

When you are familiar with the energy and feel of the disk, wait until you are having a very clear day spiritually, then prepare yourself to reestablish your link with Isis. Ancient Egyptian priestesses or priests would bathe, purify themselves with incense and flower extract oils, pray for guidance, meditate, and do whatever other personal ritual seemed appropriate.

If you have assembled the Inner Eye Power Tool, the Pink Rose, and the Grounding Disk, use them also, and any other disk that seems right for you. Then place the Isis Disk over your heart chakra and do the following meditation technique.

The Angelic Meditation Technique

This is the same technique given with the Inner Eye Disk, repeated here for your convenience. This particular meditation method is highly recommended by the Angels because it is simple, quite powerful, and with practice takes only about five minutes. It will raise your spinal energies and flood your cerebral meditation centers with psychic force. To begin, breathe deeply and slowly through your solar plexus for about two minutes.

Next, visualize or form a strong, clear idea that you are rising up out of your physical body in a body made out of pure, rich, gold light. When you are standing up in this gold body, imagine that the physical landscape is fading away, and in its place a beautiful green meadow is beginning to shimmer and take form. Fill in grass, flowers, trees, sky, birds, etc. Notice that in the center of the meadow is a large pyramid made out of brilliant white light. It has steps going up all four sides, leading to a capstone of gold light. This pyramid is about sixty feet tall, with the capstone comprising the last ten feet. Visualize that you are walking over to the pyramid in your gold body and are standing by the first step.

The point of this meditation technique is to climb the pyramid: as you climb, energy will begin to flow up your spinal column from the first (base) chakra all the way to the crown of your head. This is like raising an antenna on a TV to prepare it to receive incoming audio and visual information — only in this case, you are preparing to receive incoming thought waves and spiritual vibrations.

As you begin to climb, focus on your gold legs and take high steps. Almost immediately you should get the sensation of rising ... this tells you that the energy is beginning to flow up your spine. Climb *sixty-four steps* straight up: with the sixty-fourth step, enter into the gold light of the capstone.

Sit down and make yourself comfortable in the capstone. Let the gold light of the capstone flow through your gold body, filling it with intense energy. You should have a feeling of having climbed to a very great height. Now take a moment to visualize an eye that fills your whole mind ... this opens your third eye and prepares it for meditation.

Finding Isis

Next, take the Isis Disk from your heart chakra and hold it up to the light so you can gaze into the disk. Look carefully at Isis' features until they begin to take on life. Then gaze into her eyes, long and deeply. Isis is definitely "in there:" perhaps she will appear to smile at you, or perhaps her eyes will glitter or an eyebrow will lift. When something like that occurs, you will have connected with Isis telepathically. Listen carefully for her thoughts, which will come delicately into your mind.

When you have finished communing with Isis, put the disk back on your heart chakra and bring your gold body down all sixty-four pyramid steps and back into your physical body. If you do not climb down the pyramid your physical body will not be able to integrate the energy you have accumulated, so please don't omit this step.

The more you connect with Isis using the Master Meditation Technique, the faster you will evolve and the stronger your link with Isis will be. Sometimes after a disk session Isis comes to her former priestesses and priests in dreams, which often leads to profound past life recall.

After you have strongly reestablished your connection with Isis, she will repeat a vow she made to you long ago. If you wish, you may also repeat your ancient vow to her . . . you will remember what it was.

Healing with the Disk

The Isis Power Tool may be used on any chakra for healing purposes, and is especially powerful on the solar plexus, heart, throat, third eye, and crown chakras. If you are strobing the disk, one to two minutes will be sufficient to activate each chakra and transfer the disk's image into the auric field. If you are working by room light, it will take ten to twenty minutes per chakra. When the disk is on each chakra, inhale deeply several times and literally pull the Isis energy into your body from the disk. As the disk is working, both the healer and the client should scan for past life trauma surfacing from the chakras.

Any further information which is needed regarding old trauma will usually appear at night, frequently in the form of troubling dreams and nightmares. These should be carefully recorded and analyzed.

Egyptian Past Lives

All thoughts, psychic perceptions, or old memories which surface during an Isis session of any kind should always be carefully examined. If you use your own method to do past life regressions, it is extremely helpful to incorporate the Master Meditation Technique into your session in order to clearly access Egyptian incarnations and begin to pull up the most ancient memories. It could take several sessions to find all of the information you are seeking, but the knowledge and power that will come to you from your Egyptian lifetimes could make profound changes in your life.

Speed up your personal evolution with
POWER TOOLS

POWER TOOLS
VIBRATING HOLES IN THE WALL THAT SEPARATES US FROM THE HIGHER DIMENSIONS
OUTTA HERE!

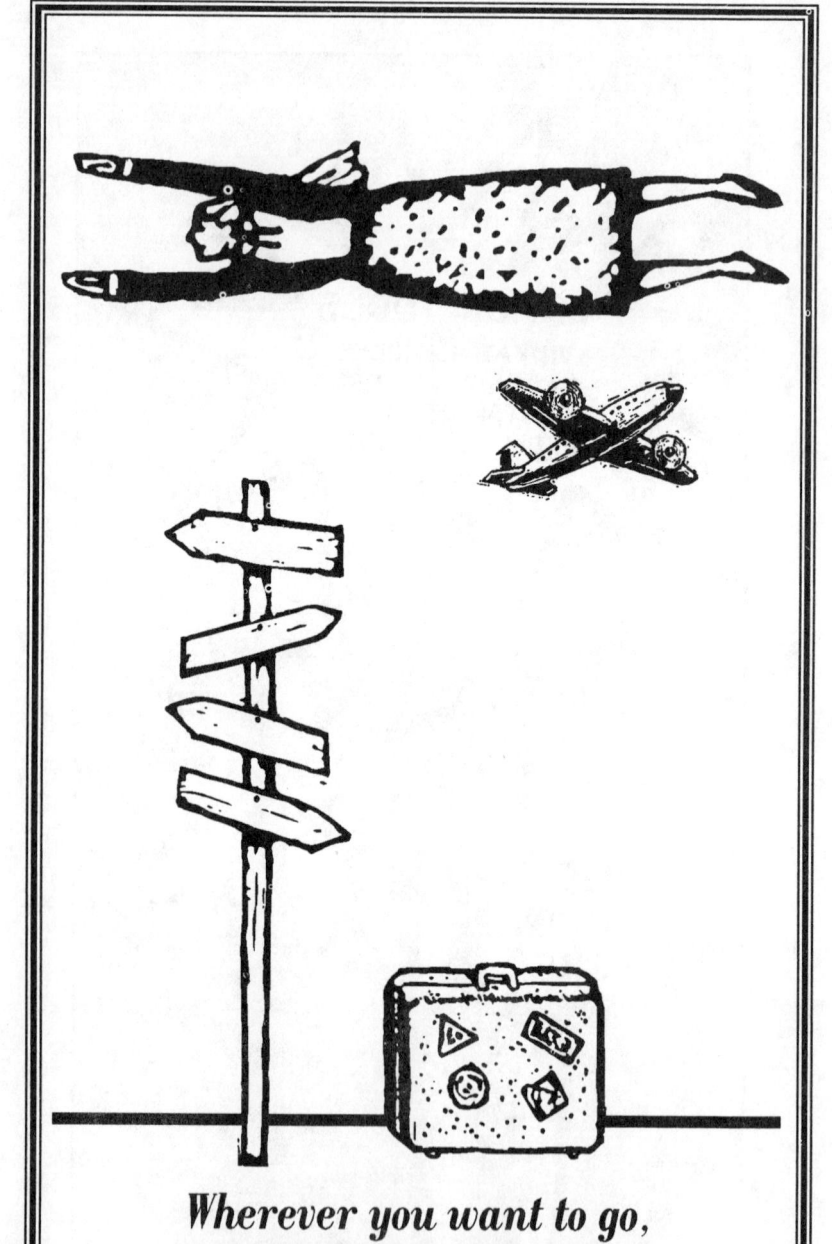

Wherever you want to go,
POWER TOOLS
will get you there.

POWER TOOLS

As good as gold... maybe even better!

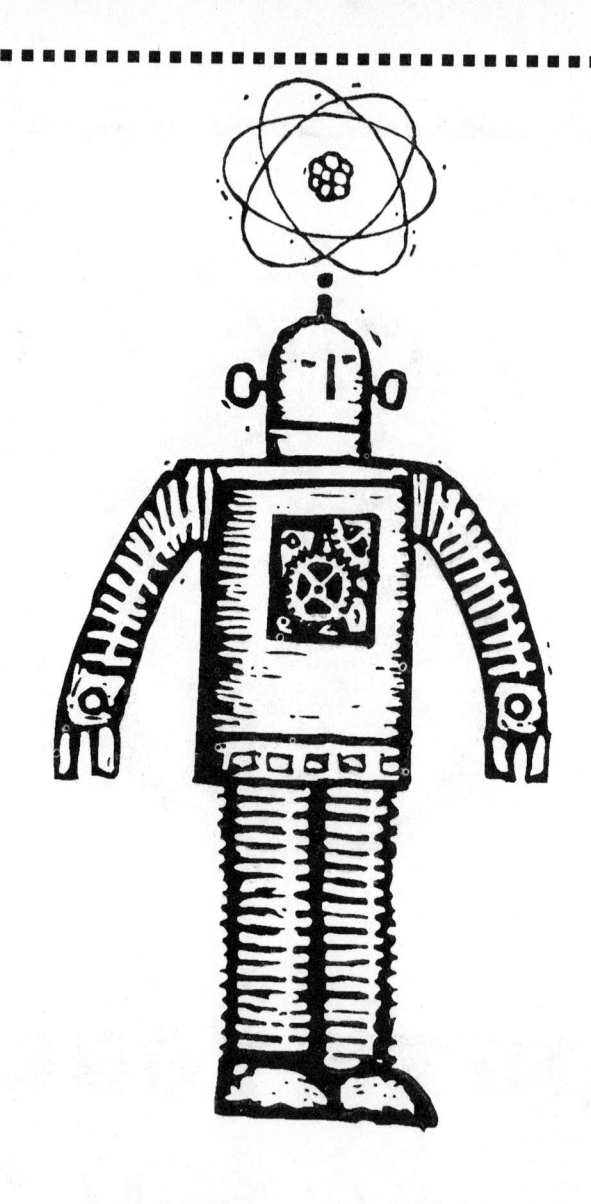

POWER TOOLS
FUTURE TECHNOLOGY
HAPPENING NOW